Kids can
Sew

Kids can Sew

Fun and easy projects for your small stitcher

Beverley Alvarez

BARRON'S

First edition for North America published
in 2004 by Barron's Educational Series, Inc.

All inquiries should be addressed to:
Barron's Educational Series, Inc.
250 Wireless Boulevard
Hauppauge, NY 11788
http://www.barronseduc.com

Library of Congress Catalog Card Number: 2003109043

International Standard Book Number: 0-7641-2771-3

A QUARTO BOOK

Copyright © 2004 Quarto Inc.

Conceived, designed, and produced by
Quarto Publishing plc
The Old Brewery
6 Blundell Street
London N7 9BH

QUAR:SFK

Project editors: Fiona Robertson and Liz Pasfield
Art editor: Anna Knight
Assistant art director: Penny Cobb
Copy editor: Claire Waite-Brown
Designer: Karin Skånberg
Illustrator: Coral Mula
Photographer: Colin Bowling
Indexer: Pamela Ellis

Art director: Moira Clinch
Publisher: Piers Spence

Manufactured by PICA Digital, Singapore
Printed by Star Standard Industries (PTE) Ltd,
Singapore

9 8 7 6 5 4 3 2 1

Contents

Introduction

Sewing is all about being creative with fabric, and it's great fun too! Learning basic sewing and embroidery stitches is not difficult, and with these simple skills under your belt you can make lots of beautiful items, from clothes and toys to bags and pillowcases. You will also be able to decorate your creations using the array of interesting beads, sequins, and ribbons available to buy today.

Kids Can Sew teaches you the techniques you want to learn and uses them to make the kind of items you'd like to sew. Once you have learned these simple skills you can use the techniques to make anything you want, such as gifts for friends and family, or treats just for you.

Hand sewing

Hand sewing is an ancient craft born both out of necessity and a desire to express a creative urge. Not only can you use hand sewing to create an item, but also to illustrate your work. Many different cultures use hand sewing as decoration to show where they come from, to tell a story, or to make something look good. It is a very useful and delightful skill that can be used in many ways. Hand sewing takes more time than machine sewing, but it is well worth the effort, so take the time to enjoy being creative with hand stitches.

Machine sewing

If you have access to a sewing machine, using it can be a quicker way to create any garment or sewn item than hand sewing. In particular, a sewing machine will allow you to make larger projects a lot more quickly. Machine stitching can also be decorative and some very modern machines include embroidery stitches. And even with a more traditional machine, a simple zigzag stitch can finish off an edge or be used as an embroidery stitch.

Learning step by step

There are loads of techniques and
15 projects to do in this
book. The best way to
learn the skills of sewing
is to follow the order of
the book, because it deals
with the easiest stitches first and builds up to
the more complicated techniques. Along the
way you will learn how to sew on buttons,
beads, and sequins for decoration; basic
embroidery stitches; how to make hems,
buttonholes, and pockets; quilting, appliqué, and smocking;
and how to line clothes and insert zippers. To
help illustrate the practicality of each new
skill you learn you can work on the various
projects, which include: finger puppets; a
reversible skirt; a hooded vest with a
fancy zipper and hidden pockets; cozy
slippers; a beautiful bag for the
evening; and a ragdoll with
some new
clothes. There is also a
section on recycling and
revamping old garments, so you can have
fun changing clothes you already own,
and learn how to make great cushion
covers out of an old pair of jeans.

The projects in this book suggest the kinds of
fabrics to use, but there are plenty of
materials of varying colors and patterns that
you might prefer to use instead, which is
just fine. And fabric does not have to be
expensive—keep any scraps and
left-over pieces; they are bound
to be useful.

Fun with friends

You can work through this
book on your own or with
other people. If you get a group of sewing
pals together you can collect and swap
fabrics, beads, ribbons, and other decorations. You may also
find it useful and encouraging to ask any experienced sewers
you know for their sewing tips, and don't be afraid to ask for
a little help if you need to. Maybe a friend or family member
would like to learn with you, because sewing can be a
fun, sharing experience. Once you have mastered
the sewing skills in this book you can help other
novice sewers get the stitching bug.

What next?

Once you know how to sew there are no
limits to what you can make. As you work
through this book you will learn to measure
yourself and to make simple patterns, after which you
will be able to use ready-made patterns. There are so
many patterns to buy, from simple toys and clothes
to adventurous ballgowns. You may want to adapt
some of the projects in the book to suit a family
member or friend. Or you could get really creative
and design your own toys, clothes, or accessories.
If you particularly like the quilting technique, for
example, why not make a complete quilt for your
bed? Or if you prefer appliqué, you could make a wall
hanging with your own choice of picture. Learning
embroidery stitches enables you to decorate any
garment or fabric household item, so there really is no
limit to the creative possibilities that learning to sew
offers you.

Getting started

The next few pages will help you get a practical sewing kit together with advice on needles, threads, and essential sewing tools. There's also a description of various fabrics to help you decide which fabric is best for your projects. You'll also find useful information on sewing by hand or machine that you can refer back to throughout the projects to remind yourself. Have fun getting your sewing kit together, collecting fabrics, and practicing your first stitches!

The sewing kit

There are a number of items that will make up your basic sewing kit, the kind of equipment you need for every sewing technique or project, such as needles, pins, scissors, and thread. Then there are some techniques that require one or two extra tools. Each project has a list of the equipment required, so always read through this list before you begin to sew and make sure you have everything close at hand. You can buy equipment from craft or sewing stores, department stores, and thrift shops. You don't have to spend a lot of money to start sewing, and if you ask around, you will probably find that people have lots of things they don't use that you could make use of.

It is a good idea to keep your sewing notions in a designated sewing box or basket. You can decorate a cardboard or plastic box if you do not have a specific sewing basket. Keep small beads, buttons, snaps, and sequins in a small jar or plastic container, and ribbons, tape, elastic, and braid in a smaller, separate container, or in plastic bags, so that the beads don't snag the ribbon. Keep needles and pins in separate small containers in your sewing box, or in a piece of felt or a pin cushion (such as the one made on pages 41–43) so that you don't prick your fingers on them when you reach into the box for something else.

The basic kit

These are the items you will always need when sewing. They are not expensive to buy and, apart from the thread, can be used over and over.

Needles

There are different types of needles to use for various sewing techniques. You will be using sewing and embroidery needles. The thing to remember is that the size of yarn or thread you use determines the size of needle you need. For this book you will need a regular sewing needle for the bulk of your sewing—this is useful even when you are sewing by machine for finishing ends off, hemming by hand, or sewing up small openings in seams. A large embroidery needle with a fine point is needed to sew yarn and thick embroidery thread, while a smaller embroidery needle with a fine point is needed for thinner embroidery thread.

Thread

To sew most fabrics you can use all-purpose mercerized thread. Match the color of the thread to the main fabric for most items and clothes, or use a color that contrasts with the fabric for an additional design feature. Cheap thread can be used for basting.

There are many different types of embroidery thread, and you will need a few assorted colors of medium-weight or lightweight embroidery thread.

Yarn can also be used for sewing, and is listed where relevant in the projects.

Button thread is needed for sewing on buttons and for extra strong stitching.

Pins

You can never have too many pins! They are used in many instances, usually to hold together two layers of fabric ready for sewing. Glass-headed pins are pretty and easy to pick up.

Scissors

Large, sharp scissors are needed for cutting out fabric, while small pointed scissors are best for snipping threads, cutting buttonholes, and trimming seams.

Safety pins

Large and small safety pins are needed for threading elastic or ribbon through casings, and they are also useful for holding things in place.

Tailor's chalk

This is used for making removable marks on fabric, to clearly show you where to cut out the lines of a pattern or where to sew on decorations, for example. Tailor's chalk can be bought in different colors. White is used for most fabrics but a color can be useful if you are working with light-colored fabrics.

Tape measure

A tape measure is a necessity. Make sure it has U.S. or metric measurements on it but stick to one or the other to avoid confusion.

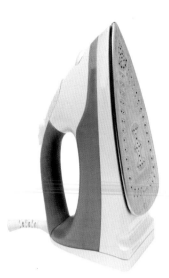

Useful extras

The following tools are used in some of the projects in this book, so remember to read the materials list for each project and arm yourself with some of these extras if necessary.

Fabric pens

These are pens designed for drawing onto fabrics. Ironing on the reverse of the fabric after using the pens will make the drawing permanent. Remember to use the right iron setting for your fabric.

Knitting needle or stick with rounded ends

This is very useful for pushing batting into small areas.

Iron and ironing board

Although not strictly speaking a part of the basic sewing kit, you will need to use an iron on your main fabrics and finished items. An iron with various settings is used for pressing fabrics before you start sewing, and for pressing seams open so they lie flat. An iron becomes very hot so be extra careful when you use one. Ask an adult if you can use the iron, and ask her to supervise you the first few times. The ironing board should stand firmly and have a smooth, fitted cover. A board with adjustable height is useful.

Pressing cloth

A 2 foot (60 cm) square of finely woven cotton is essential for steam pressing. Place it over the fabric to protect it from the direct heat of the iron. Wash it first to remove any sizing.

Ironing and ironing safety

● Ironing and pressing are done on the wrong side of the fabric whenever possible. With cotton fabrics it is fine to iron right onto the fabric, but with synthetic and wool fabrics a pressing cloth is needed.

● Make sure you have the right setting for your fabric.

● Use a cool/medium setting for synthetic fabrics and a damp pressing cloth if the material is very creased.

● Use a medium/hot setting for cotton, linen, silk, and wool, and a damp pressing cloth if the fabric is very creased.

● Be careful not to stretch the fabric as you iron.

● Scorch marks and burns are very difficult to get out, so start ironing with a cool setting and test on a piece of spare fabric if possible.

● The sole plate needs to be kept clean so that it doesn't leave marks on the fabric. Iron cleaners can be purchased, but rubbing lemon juice on the sole plate can also remove marks.

● Keep your hands away from the hot sole plate.

Pattern cutting paper

This paper has an all-over grid either in U.S. or metric measurements. The grid helps you to transfer your measurements accurately onto the paper to make a pattern. You can make your own by drawing an accurate grid of squares (all the same size) over large sheets of thin paper or tracing paper.

Pencil

A soft pencil should be used for drawing on pattern cutting paper.

Yardstick (meter) or ruler

A straight edge is used for connecting points together and measuring hems.

Seam ripper

A seam ripper is used for removing basting stitches and turning under seam allowances.

Embroidery hoop

An embroidery hoop holds the fabric between two circles, one inner circle that the fabric goes over and a slightly larger circle to fix over the smaller one. Move for each area you need to embroider.

Nonessential extras

The following tools are not absolutely necessary to complete the projects in this book, but if you get the bug and know you want to do a lot of sewing, you may want to invest in them.

Magnet

A magnet is not essential but if you have one it is a useful piece of equipment to pick up dropped pins and needles.

Thimble

A thimble fitted on the middle finger of your sewing hand directs and pushes the needle through the fabric. It may seem clumsy using one at first but if you are hand sewing it can save sore fingers!

Fabrics

Choosing fabric can be quite overwhelming! There are so many different types, colors, and patterns available to buy. Using the right type of fabric for the kind of item you want to make is quite important, so read through the following list for useful information on what to use and how to care for different fabrics. The projects in this book suggest the best type of fabric to use. If you buy ready-made patterns you will find suggestions for the type of fabric and the amount you will need written on the back of the pattern envelope.

Cottons and cotton/polyester blends

Cotton comes from the ripe, fluffy seedpod of the cotton plant. Polyester is a man-made fiber. Some cotton fabrics contain mixed fibers of cotton and polyester.

Cotton and cotton/poly blends are ideal for craft projects and clothing. You can buy cotton and cotton/poly blends in any color and many different designs. These fabrics are easy to sew and wash well. You can get different weights, from thin, lightweight to thicker, heavyweight. If you are using interfacing use a weight to match the main fabric.

Cotton and cotton/poly blends can be pressed with a medium to hot iron. Wash all fabrics first to remove excess dye and sizing—this will also shrink the fabric before you sew the garment—then press the fabric well with a medium to hot iron before use.

The following are all examples of cottons or cotton/poly blends, often referred to by specific names.

Light to medium-weight cottons

Light to medium-weight cottons are used for clothes, bed linen, toys, accessories, and appliqué. They are easy to use and wash well. These fabrics are available in a multitude of colors and designs.

Denim

Denim is a light or heavyweight, very strong cotton fabric. It can be bought in dark to light shades. Some denim has been washed to give it a worn or faded look.

Gingham

Gingham is a yarn-dyed plain weave cotton fabric in stripes, plaids, or checks.

Interfacing

Interfacing is used to back the fabric of a garment to help stiffen and strengthen certain areas. It comes in various weights and can be iron-on or sew-in. Buy the right weight to suit your main fabric.

Napped or piled fabrics

The nap of the fabric is a design or pattern that runs the same direction down or across the fabric. The pile is the finish of the right side of the fabric. It has short or long fibers running down the length of the fabric. You need to take extra care when cutting out these materials, making sure the nap or pile faces in the same direction on all the pieces.

Press with a cool to medium iron on the reverse on a clean, dry towel, to avoid flattening the pile. Follow the washing instructions.

Napped or piled fabrics include:

Terry cloth

This is a soft absorbent cotton fabric with closely woven loops on one or both sides.

Velvet

Velvet can be man-made or made from natural fibers. It has a thick pile that gives a smooth, luxurious finish. Some velvets are washable but others are not, so ask in the store where you buy the fabric for washing care instructions.

Corduroy

This fabric has a short pile like velvet, in wide or narrow strips running down the length of the fabric. Corduroy is particularly good for clothes and accessories.

Fun fur fabric

Fun fur fabrics can have a short or long pile and have a knitted backing. There are many different designs and colors to choose from. Fun fur can be difficult to sew but there is a technique to it (see page 107).

Silky fabrics

Silky fabrics can be man-made or made from natural fibers. Silky fabrics can be used for lining, clothes, and accessories. They range from lightweight to heavyweight. If you are using interfacing use a weight to match the main fabric.

Silky fabrics should be pressed with a cool to medium iron. Wash in warm water and iron when damp. Use a pressing cloth and steam iron if the fabric is not damp.

Here are the main silky fabrics you are likely to find:

Silk

Silk is a natural fiber that comes from the filament spun by the silkworm for its cocoon. It can be a flat weave or have an uneven slub running through the weave of the fabric. When cutting out, place the pattern pieces on the "nap" of the fabric (see page 15).

Satin

Satin is shiny on the right side of the fabric and can be made from natural or man-made fibers. This is a medium-weight fabric, perfect for clothes and accessories. Also used for lining.

Polyester and acetate silky fabric

Synthetic silky fabrics made from polyester or acetate are very similar to the natural-fiber silky fabrics, although they are usually cheaper and easy to sew. These are often used for lining.

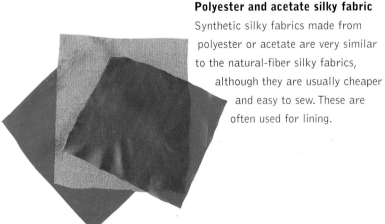

Woolen and fleece fabrics

There are lots of different wools, from light to heavyweight. Ask for washing instructions when you buy the fabric. Press carefully with a steam iron or damp pressing cloth. Fleece is easy to wash but be careful pressing as a hot iron leaves marks.

Woolen or fleece fabrics include:

Felt

Felt is made from compressed wool fibers rather than woven wool. It is not good for clothes but ideal for toys, bags, accessories, and craft projects and is easy to sew. Do not wash.

Fleece

This can be bought in many colors and designs, and is used for many outerwear garments and accessories.

Wool

Lightweight wool can be used for clothes. A lining is usually used in garments made from wool.

PVC fabric

PVC fabric can be bought with a fabric backing with a strong plastic film on top, or with no backing. PVC is available in many colors and textures as well as clear, by the yard or meter. It is better to use a medium-weight fabric since thin PVC may tear when sewn. Do not press PVC fabric.

Sew PVC fabric with a Teflon sewing machine foot. If sewing by hand a thimble may be needed. This is a good fabric to use for details on accessories, bags, and some simple clothes.

Measuring for clothes

To ensure that clothes fit properly you will need to be able to measure yourself, or the person the clothes are for, in the correct way. There are a few essential measurements that you need to take for simple garments.

Tape measures often have both U.S. measurements (inches and yards) and metric measurements (centimeters and meters) printed on them. Stick to one type of measurement only, either U.S. or metric, because using both will get confusing.

Where to measure

Here is a diagram of the most important measurements you need to take when you want to make clothes. Have your tape measure and a pen and paper ready before you begin measuring. Lengths can be difficult to measure, so ask someone to help if needed, and remember to stand up straight. Do not measure too tightly, but allow the tape measure to run closely over you. Keep a note of your measurements and you can refer to them whenever you need to.

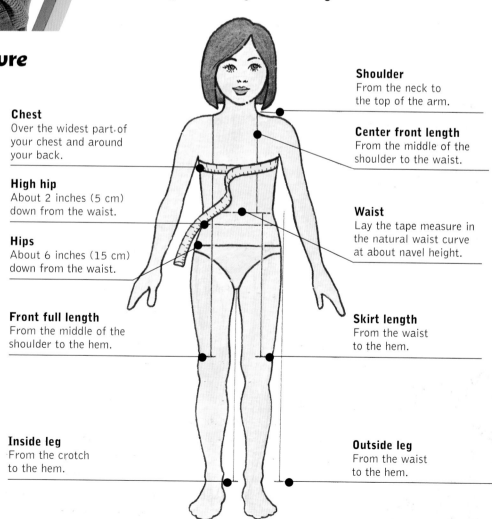

Chest
Over the widest part of your chest and around your back.

High hip
About 2 inches (5 cm) down from the waist.

Hips
About 6 inches (15 cm) down from the waist.

Front full length
From the middle of the shoulder to the hem.

Inside leg
From the crotch to the hem.

Shoulder
From the neck to the top of the arm.

Center front length
From the middle of the shoulder to the waist.

Waist
Lay the tape measure in the natural waist curve at about navel height.

Skirt length
From the waist to the hem.

Outside leg
From the waist to the hem.

Basic hand stitches

Here are some easy-to-follow steps and illustrations for basic hand stitching. Practice the stitches on scraps of fabric. Don't worry if you make a few mistakes, you can practice again before starting the first easy projects!

Threading a needle

Before you begin to make any stitches you need to thread your needle correctly.

1 Thread the needle with about 20 inches (50 cm) of thread, since any longer may get tangled. Moisten and flatten one end of the thread between your lips, then push it carefully through the needle's eye.

2 Pull the ends of the thread together, so the thread is doubled up, and tie them together in a knot.

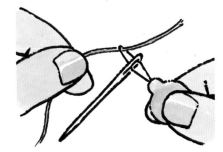

3 You can also use a needle threader which has a pointed loop to help you get the thread through the eye of the needle.

Basting

The basting stitch is the first stitch you will learn. Basting stitches are temporary stitches that hold two or more fabrics together after pinning and before the final stitching. It is basically a large, loose running stitch. As this won't be seen on the final garment or item it doesn't matter if it isn't very neat!

1 To practice this stitch, place two pieces of fabric together and pin in position.

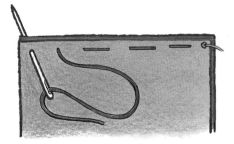

2 You only need a single thread for the basting stitch. Just pull a little of the thread through the eye of the needle. Then tie a knot at the other end.

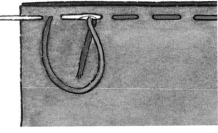

3 Start at one end of the seam allowance and keep the needle level as you push it in and out of the material, making straight, medium-sized stitches evenly spaced to the end of the pinned row. The stitches should be about ¼ inch (6 mm) long and spaced ¼ inch (6 mm) apart. Do not pull the thread too tight or stretch the fabric.

4 Finish off with a backstitch (see page 19).

5 Now you can remove the pins and the basting will keep the two fabrics together while you sew the seams. You can then remove the basting stitch after the seams have been sewn.

Running stitch

The running stitch is the stitch you will use most often, for sewing fabrics together and for decorative embroidery. To sew fabrics together, thread a sewing needle with a double length of sewing thread. If you are using the running stitch decoratively, thread an embroidery needle with a single length of embroidery thread and knot one end.

1 Bring the needle up through the fabric from the back. Make straight stitches by weaving the needle point in and out of the fabric or layers of fabric. Weave the needle through the fabric several times before pulling it through.

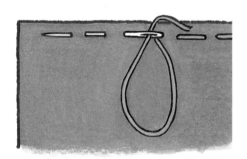

2 The stitches should be small and evenly spaced, about ⅛ inch (3 mm) long and ⅛ inch (3 mm) apart.

Overcasting

Overcast stitches run along and over the edge of a seam. A few overcast stitches can also hold a piece of ribbon or other decoration in place.

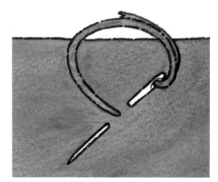

1 Work from right to left. Thread a double length of sewing thread or a single length of embroidery thread. Bring the needle through from the back of the fabric about ⅛ inch (3 mm) down from the edge.

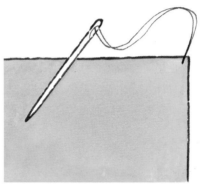

2 Take the needle over the edge of the fabric and back through about ¼ inch (6 mm) along. Repeat. Do not pull the stitches too tightly since this will pucker the fabric.

Backstitch

Backstitch is an embroidery stitch used for fine lines and details. Thread the embroidery needle with embroidery thread and tie a knot at one end.

1 Bring the needle through to the right side of the fabric and make a small backward stitch. Bring the needle back up through the fabric about ⅛–¼ inch (3–6 mm) in front of the first stitch.

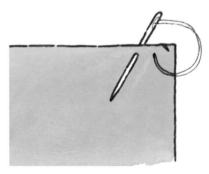

2 Make another backward stitch to the start of the last stitch. Bring the needle out ⅛–¼ inch (3–6 mm) in front of the stitch as before. Continue along the stitching line.

Using a sewing machine

You don't have to own a sewing machine to complete the projects in this book, but using one can make light work of large sewing jobs. With a sewing machine you can sew all sorts of items in many sizes with fast results. Many sewing machines can be adjusted so that they sew zigzag and embroidery stitches, and you can buy special presser feet for different tasks. Some machines have special hemming feet that sew a narrow hem in one operation, saving you the chore of pinning and basting first. Read your machine's instruction book thoroughly to see what it can do!

All sewing machines have a top thread, which feeds into the needle from the top of the machine, and a bobbin thread, which drops into the machine under the needle. When you are using the machine correctly the top thread will show on top of the fabric and the bobbin thread will show on the bottom of the material. The two threads interlock to make the stitches.

Knowing your way around a sewing machine

Although there are many different makes of sewing machine to choose from, they all work in much the same way. Here is a useful list of sewing machine parts, but remember that your machine may vary so read its manual before you begin sewing. You may want to read the instruction manual with an adult, who will be able to help you thread the machine and carry out the first few stitches.

Successful machine sewing

● If the thread underneath is loopy, check that the needle is the correct way around, and adjust the bobbin tension. Also make sure the top thread is running through the correct hooks and between the tension discs.

● If the thread keeps breaking try loosening the tension.

● Remember to use the right size of needle and stitch to suit your choice of fabric—a lightweight fabric needs a fine needle and small stitches, while a heavyweight fabric requires a thicker needle and long stitches. Stretch fabrics need a stretch stitch if possible, so use a narrow zigzag of medium length.

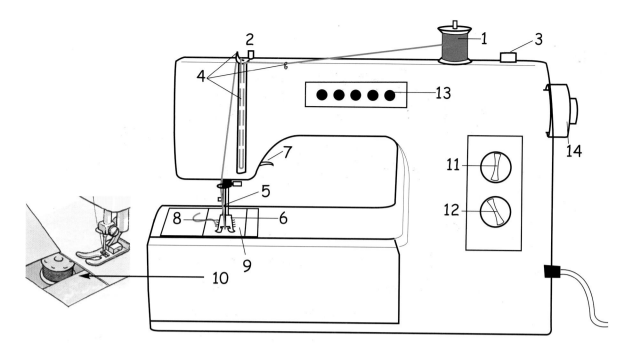

1 Thread spindle/spool pin The top thread is placed here.

2 Thread tension guide This is adjusted to keep the thread at the correct tension, so it doesn't snap or loop when stitching.

3 Bobbin winder This is used when winding bobbins. Check your instruction book for directions.

4 Upper thread guides These hooks or loops are for the top thread.

5 Needle This is held in place with a screw. Make sure you put the needle in correctly. Check the instruction book for information. Sewing machine needles come in different sizes and you need to use a size that suits the thickness of the fabric you use. A fine needle is suitable for thin fabrics and a thicker needle for heavyweight fabric.

6 Presser foot Used to hold the fabric flat as it is fed through the machine.

7 Presser foot lever Used to raise and lower the presser foot.

8 Feed dogs These help the fabric through as it is stitched.

9 Throat plate or needle plate This fits over the feed dogs and usually has markings to indicate seam allowance distances from the needle position. The needle goes down through the throat plate opening to meet the bobbin thread and make the stitches.

10 Bobbin and bobbin case Wind thread onto the bobbin for the underneath thread. The bobbin is either dropped into the case or the case is removed and the bobbin is inserted.

11 Stitch length The stitch length can be altered from small to large using a dial or lever. The choice of stitch length depends on the fabric and the type of stitching—smaller stitches for thin fabric and larger for thicker fabric.

12 Stitch width The stitch width of zigzag or decorative stitching can be increased or decreased.

13 Stitch selection Turn a dial or press a button to select a stitch. Check the tension of the stitch on a spare piece of fabric before sewing.

14 Flywheel Used to raise and lower the needle slowly.

15 Foot control (not shown) Pressed by foot to control the stitching.

Maintenance and safety

● Look after your machine! Oil it lightly—the instruction book will illustrate where the oil points are and suggest how often you should oil it. Wipe away any excess oil before sewing.

● Always turn the machine off at the switch when you finish sewing or if you have any problems.

● Keep your fingers out of the way of the moving needle.

Techniques

Threading the sewing machine

Getting to know how to use your machine saves costly mistakes later. You'll need to read your machine's manual to help you start, but you may also find that the step-by-step text and illustrations below help you make sense of the process.

1 Wind the thread around the bobbin a few times, and clip the bobbin onto the winder. Fill with thread following the manufacturer's instructions. If the thread winds loosely or unevenly the bobbin can jam. Use the same thread in the top thread and the bobbin.

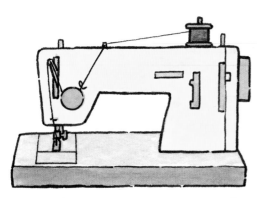

2 The instruction book will tell you exactly how to thread your machine, but it will look a lot like this illustration. It is important that the machine is threaded correctly or it will not stitch properly.

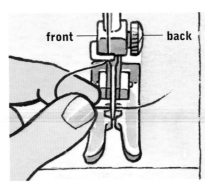

front — back

3 The machine needle is usually threaded from front to back. Trim the end of the thread, moisten it, and pass it through the needle's eye.

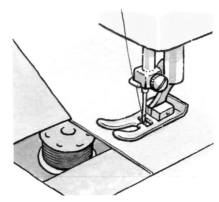

4 Put the wound bobbin into the bobbin case. Using the flywheel, lower the threaded needle and draw up the bobbin thread.

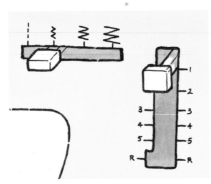

5 Select the type of stitch you need, for example straight or zigzag. Adjust the length and width if necessary.

Machine stitching

Once again, you will find that the machine's booklet tells you how to use your sewing machine, so read the instructions first, then have some fun practicing all the stitches.

Safety

● **Remember to keep your fingers away from the moving needle to avoid accidents.**

● **If anything goes wrong, switch off the machine right away and ask an adult to help you consult the instruction manual and fix the error.**

1 Check that you are comfortable sitting at the machine and that it is at a good height. Put cushions on your chair and use a foot stool if necessary. Make sure you are also close to a good light source.

2 Thread the machine and bobbin according to the instruction booklet, and look at the previous steps for advice. Select the kind of stitching you require and get some scrap fabric to practice on. Always test the stitching first on a spare piece of fabric to see if the size and tension work properly.

3 Place the material under the presser foot and lower the foot. Start the first stitches using the flywheel, turning it slowly and holding both threads at the back to stop them or the edge of the fabric from being pulled down into the throat plate.

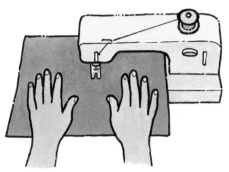

4 Then start the machine by pressing on the foot control. Practice guiding the material under the presser foot, but do not push or pull it. Start sewing slowly when you use the foot control until you get used to the speed. Take your foot away from the foot control when you stop sewing. And remember to keep your fingers away from the needle.

5 Machine stitches should be even on both sides of the material. If they are looped on one side, or break easily, consult an adult and the machine's instruction book to find out where you are going wrong. Refer to page 20 for remedies to some common problems.

6 To sew around corners, stop at the corner with the needle down. Raise the presser foot and turn the material. Lower the foot and continue stitching.

7 To sew curved edges, guide the material around gently while you sew.

8 Finish by using the reverse button for a short distance, then stop and snip off the thread ends.

Machine buttonholes

This is how you should sew buttonholes on a sewing machine. Remember to practice on a spare piece of fabric.

1 Use tailor's chalk to mark the length of buttonhole you require on the right side of the fabric. Baste close to the drawn line down both sides.

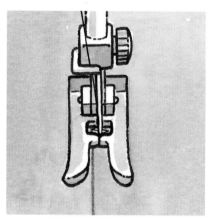

2 Thread the machine and set it to a small to medium width, short length zigzag stitch. Start at one end of the line and, keeping one edge of the zigzag stitch on the drawn line, sew to the end.

3 Sew up the other side of the drawn line in the same way, leaving a narrow gap between the lines of stitching. Take care not to overlap the stitches when sewing.

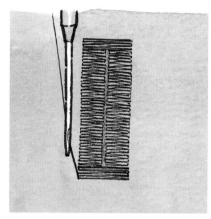

4 Sew a bar tack over the ends of the buttonhole—this is simply made up of a few zigzag stitches.

5 Using sharp pointed scissors, snip between the zigzag stitching to the bar tacks. Be careful not to snip through any stitches.

Fun projects

Here are some great projects for you to make! Work through the book and learn all the techniques. They will be useful for your future sewing projects. You can make a sparkly belt using the first simple stitches. The reversible skirt is so easy you'll surprise yourself with how good you are at sewing. After making the embroidered pillowcase and cute slippers you can put your feet up before starting the other projects. Continue through the book and you'll have a great collection of toys, garments, and accessories. Don't worry if things go wrong, you can always try again. Have fun and be creative!

Starting and finishing

First things first! Launching right into the stitching could be disastrous if you have not first learned about patterns and seam allowances, and how to finish your stitches securely. So grab paper and pencil, scissors, a few scraps of fabric, and the sewing thread and needle you will find in any sewing kit, however small, and let's get started with the basics.

Preparing the fabric

The first thing to do is press out any creases in the fabric with an iron, referring back to the pressing instructions on page 12. An adult can help or do this for you if you prefer.

Seam allowance

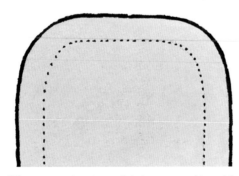

When you cut out any fabric you need to add a seam allowance all around. This is usually about ½–¾ inch (1.25–2 cm) for clothes and most toys, and it gives you the space you need to sew up the seams. When you are making a pattern from paper, remember to include this extra measurement.

Using a paper pattern

1 To practice using a paper pattern, first cut out any simple shape from a sheet of pattern paper.

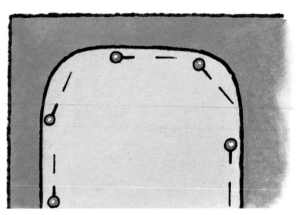

2 Pin the paper pattern onto the back of the fabric. To check that the pattern is running the correct way for the fabric, look at the information about fabric on pages 14–16. Use enough pins to secure well, just inside the edge of the pattern.

3 Cut around the pattern, then take the pins out.

Threading the needle

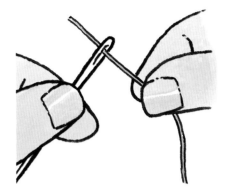  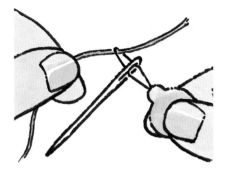

1 Thread the needle with about 20 inches (50 cm) of thread. To do this, moisten and flatten one end of the thread between your lips, then push it through the needle's eye.

2 Pull the thread through so you can tie the ends in a knot. If you only need a single thread just pull a little of the thread through the eye, then tie a knot at the other end of the thread.

3 You can also use a needle threader which has a pointed loop to help you get the thread through the eye of the needle.

Finishing stitching

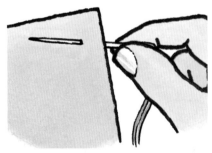

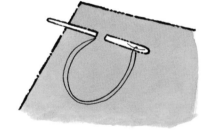

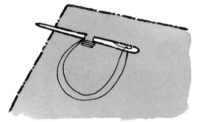

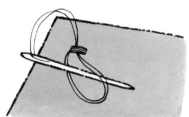

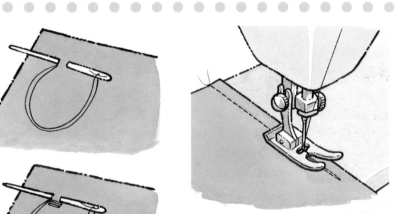

1 To practice finishing you need to make a few stitches. Thread the needle as above, then push it through the fabric from the back.

2 Push the needle in and out of the fabric to make a few stitches. Don't worry about the look of the stitches at this stage.

3 **Top** Finish the stitches off at the back of your fabric by sewing through a small piece of the fabric.
Middle Overcast a few small stitches.
Bottom Sew through your stitches and the loop before you pull your thread tight. Trim your thread near to the stitches.

4 For machine stitching, simply reverse a few stitches and trim the thread.

Techniques

Sewing things on

Before you begin sewing two pieces of fabric together, you can practice working with a needle and thread by sewing buttons and beads onto any fabric. Then, when you come to the projects, you will see how buttons and beads are used to decorate plain fabrics.

Buttons and beads

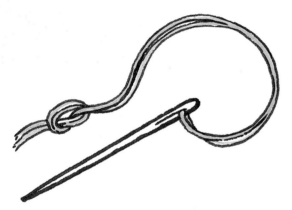

1 Thread the needle as shown on page 27.

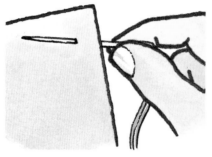

2 Push the threaded needle through the fabric from the back to the front, so the knot is underneath.

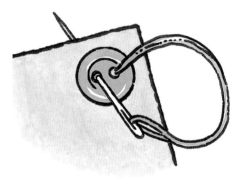

5 With a button, push the needle and thread down through the other hole and straight through the fabric. Repeat steps 4 and 5 twice. Make sure the needle is at the back of the fabric, underneath the button.

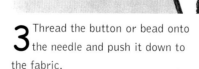

3 Thread the button or bead onto the needle and push it down to the fabric.

4 Pull the needle up through the fabric and button or bead.

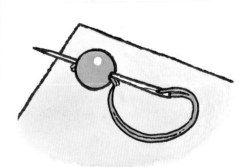

6 Sew beads in the same way as buttons, but sew through the bead from side to side.

Finishing off

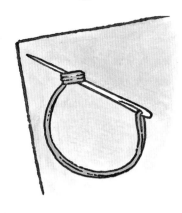

1 To finish off, first thread the needle through the stitches at the back of the button or bead, but do not pull it tight yet.

2 Pass the needle through the loop you have just made, then pull it tight. Trim the thread close to the stitches.

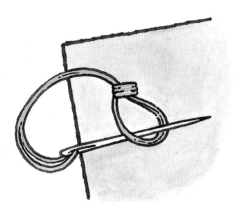

Snaps

A snap is like a button and buttonhole, and is used to join two pieces of fabric together. There are two parts to a snap that stay together when pressed. Sew one part of the snap to the first piece of fabric and the other to a second piece.

1 Thread the needle and position one half of the snap on the fabric.

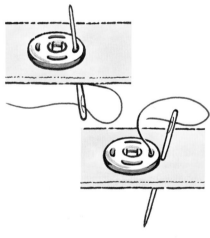

2 Bring the needle up through one of the holes on the snap, over the side, and down through the fabric. Then come up through the next snap hole. Repeat around all the holes.

3 Finish off at the back of the fabric as you did with buttons and beads.

4 Position the other side of the snap at the matching point on a second piece of fabric, sew in the same way.

Sequins

1 All the sequins on one item should be sewn in the same direction as each other. Thread the needle and place the first sequin on the fabric.

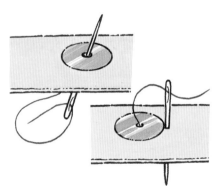

2 Starting from the back, sew up through the fabric and sequin. Push the needle back through the fabric over the side of the sequin.

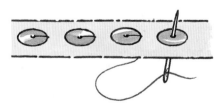

3 You can add as many sequins, and place them as close together, as you like. One stitch is enough for each sequin. You do not need to finish off behind each one if you are sewing on a few close together. Sew up through the next sequin as before.

4 Finish off at the back of the last sequin as usual.

Buckles

1 First make sure your buckle fits the size of your strap. Do this by measuring your strap and the middle pin of your buckle.

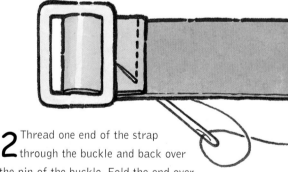

2 Thread one end of the strap through the buckle and back over the pin of the buckle. Fold the end over twice, about 1 inch (2.5 cm) away from the buckle. Fasten by sewing along the edge along the underside of the strap.

Bejeweled belt

This belt shows the result that can be had from simply decorating fabric with buttons, beads, and sequins. And because snaps are so easy to sew on, you'll find yourself wanting to make more and more.

This project only uses the skills you have learned so far, but if you have forgotten any, go back to the techniques pages to remind yourself.

Heart-felt belt loop

Making the heart

1 On paper, draw a heart shape that is about 3½ inches (9 cm) wide at the top. Then cut it out.

⚠ Cut out two hearts from your felt.

2 Use the paper heart pattern to cut out two felt hearts. Cut another heart shape that is about ¼ inch (6 mm) smaller than the felt shape, from cardboard.

Beautiful beading!

30

Materials

● Approximately 8 inch (20 cm) square of felt

● Decorations: buttons; beads; sequins

● Sewing thread to match the buttons, beads, and sequins

● Embroidery thread, your choice of color

● 5 inches (13 cm) of thin ribbon

● Sewing needle

● Embroidery needle

● Scissors, paper, and pencil

● Thin cardboard

● Small snap

▲ Sew on your ribbon.

3 Sew one end of your ribbon to the back of one heart shape near the top in the middle.

▲ You can decorate your heart with as many sequins as you like.

4 Sew a fancy button or bead on the other felt heart shape. Add more beads or sequins if desired.

▲ Don't forget to leave a gap big enough for your cardboard heart.

5 Place the top felt heart shape over the back felt heart, making sure that the ribbon is on the outside. Sew around the edge with a simple small running stitch using embroidery thread. Make sure you leave a gap big enough at one side to slide your heart shape cardboard into.

▲ When both snaps have been sewn on you will have a loop for your heart.

6 Insert your cardboard heart into your felt heart and sew up the remainder of the seam. Then sew half of your snap to the loose end of your ribbon, facing outward. Sew the other half on the ribbon on the back of the heart.

 Project 1

Beautiful beading!

Materials

● 1 inch (2.5 cm) wide ribbon or thick cotton twill tape, enough length to go around your waist or hips, plus 8 inches (20 cm) extra to thread through the buckle

- - - - - - - - - - - - - - - -

● 1 inch (2.5 cm) buckle

- - - - - - - - - - - - - - - -

● Decorations: buttons; beads; long beads for the fringe; small round beads for the end of the fringe

- - - - - - - - - - - - - - - -

● Sewing thread to match the buttons and beads

- - - - - - - - - - - - - - - -

● Sewing needle

- - - - - - - - - - - - - - - -

● Scissors

- - - - - - - - - - - - - - - -

● Tailor's chalk

- - - - - - - - - - - - - - - -

Fringe benefits

Making the belt

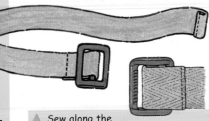

▲ Sew along the edge of the twice-folded tape or ribbon to secure the buckle.

1 Turn over the tip of one end of the ribbon or tape, folding in twice toward the inside. Sew along the edge to secure.

2 Loop the other end through the buckle, fold over twice toward the inside (not too close to the buckle), and sew along the edge.

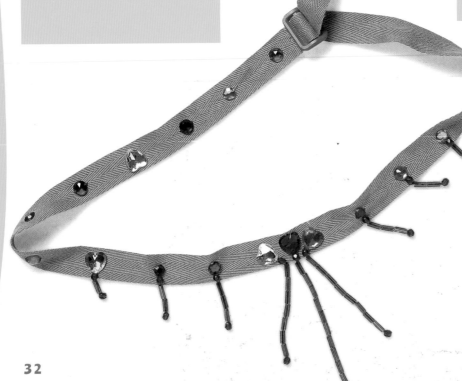

Decorating the belt

1 Lay the belt flat with the front side facing you. Measure 9 inches (23 cm) in from the non-buckle end. Between here and the buckle, decide where you want to position the buttons or beads and mark with tailor's chalk. This belt closes at the side with the fringe off-center, but you can have the buckle at the front and the fringe all around.

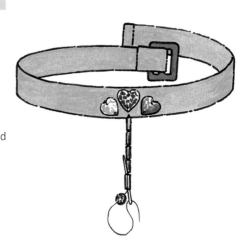

▲ Add as many beads as you like to make the fringe of the belt.

2 Sew on the buttons or beads in the marked positions. To make the fringe, simply start from the belt with a few stitches and add long beads to your thread, using a small bead at the end to finish.

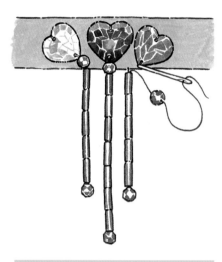

▲ Add a bead on the top of each fringe and finish off at the back of the belt.

3 Sew around the small bead, then back up through the long beads, adding another small bead onto the belt at the top. Finish off at the back.

Now you have a really cool belt and charm. Try making one for a friend, remembering to measure around his or her waist or hips so that it will fit perfectly.

33

The first stitches

Basting is the first stitch you will learn. It is a large running stitch that holds fabrics together before the final stitching. Overcasting is also a useful stitch to learn. Next, you can have some fun learning a few popular embroidery stitches. Embroidery is a great way to decorate fabric. Once you have the hang of these stitches there's a great project which puts them into practice.

Using a thread that contrasts in color with the fabric means that the stitches are clearly visible.

Basting

1 To practice this stitch, place two pieces of fabric together and pin in position.

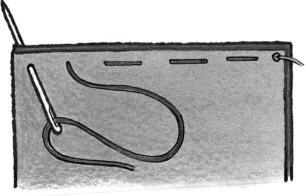

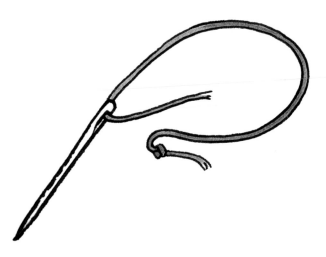

2 Thread a sewing needle with a single sewing thread and tie a knot at one end.

3 Keep the needle flat and push it in and out of the material, making long, loose, straight stitches. Don't worry if the stitches aren't the same size. This stitch will be taken out later, so it won't be seen.

4 After basting two pieces of fabric together, finish off with one overcast stitch. You don't have to finish off securely because you will remove the basting later.

5 Remove the pins and the basting will keep the two fabrics together while you sew the seams. Remove the basting after the final stitching. Materials like leather, PVC, or suede should be held together with masking tape instead of basting because they might show pin marks.

Overcasting

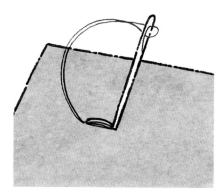

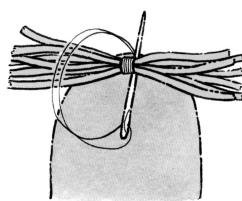

For a simple overcast stitch, thread your needle and start at the back of your fabric or, if sewing on hair for a soft toy, on the top where the hair will be. Sew an overcast stitch by pulling the needle up through the fabric, over and back through the fabric. Sew a few stitches in the same place. Finish off at the back. If sewing on hair, catch the strands of yarn in the stitches. Finish off underneath the hair.

Running stitch

1 Thread an embroidery needle with embroidery thread and tie a knot at one end.

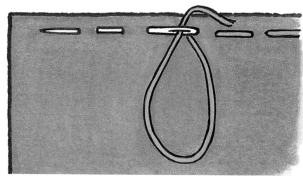

2 Keep the needle flat and push it in and out of the material, making a line of small, equal stitches and spaces.

3 Finish off at the back (see finishing stitching on page 27).

Backstitch

1 Thread the embroidery needle with embroidery thread and tie a knot at one end.

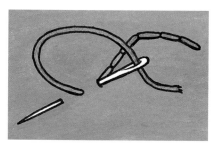

2 Sew through the fabric from the back and make a small straight stitch. Bring the needle up through the fabric and back down at the end of the last stitch. Repeat to make a row of connected stitches.

3 To finish off backstitch, sew over to the last stitch, do not sew back up through your fabric. Finish off at the back.

Backstitch is a good stitch for writing. Write your initials on a practice cloth with tailor's chalk, then embroider it using backstitch.

Techniques

Blanket stitch

This stitch is worked along the edge of the fabric, from left to right.

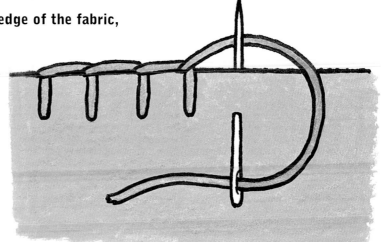

1 Thread the embroidery needle with embroidery thread and tie a knot at one end.

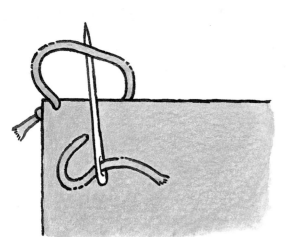

2 Start from the left to the right. With the edge of your fabric facing up, start sewing by pushing your needle through the fabric to the right side. Then push your needle through the fabric slightly further along and bring out at the edge under the thread. Pull gently.

3 ▲ Take the needle right through the fabric and draw it out in front of the thread that lies along the top edge. Do not pull or pucker the stitch.

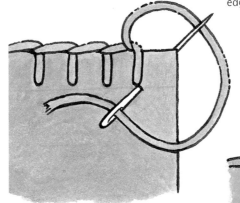

4 To work around a corner, put the needle in at the bottom of the last stitch. Bring it out at the corner. Secure with a small, extra stitch. Start the next stitch at the corner.

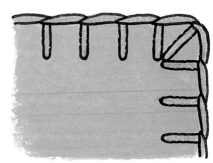

5 To finish off, sew over the thread and bring your needle over to the back, finish off in the usual way. This is a very useful stitch for buttonholes and edging.

With just these few stitches under your belt you can make all kinds of great things. Just look at the next two projects!

Fun finger puppets

With this easy project you can use some of the embroidery techniques you have just learned to make a family of cute finger puppets and pets. Once you have made enough for one hand, you can use your own ideas to make characters for the other hand. What about wild animals or crazy monsters?

This project uses the sewing skills you have already learned. But if you need to be reminded of any of the techniques, simply look back at the illustrations and instructions on the techniques pages.

Materials

- Two 6 inch (15 cm) squares of felt, a different color for each animal

- - - - - - - - - - - - - - -

- Decorations: 2 small buttons; 2 tiny beads

- - - - - - - - - - - - - - -

- Sewing thread to match the buttons and beads

- - - - - - - - - - - - - - -

- Embroidery thread in a contrasting color to the felt

- - - - - - - - - - - - - - -

- Sewing needle

- - - - - - - - - - - - - - -

- Embroidery needle

- - - - - - - - - - - - - - -

- Scissors

- - - - - - - - - - - - - - -

- Ruler

- - - - - - - - - - - - - - -

- Tailor's chalk

- - - - - - - - - - - - - - -

Finger puppet cat and mouse

Making the cat

1 Cut out two 3 x 2 inch (7.5 x 5 cm) rectangles from the felt you have chosen for the cat.

▲ Draw a horizontal line across the felt. Make sure the tailor's chalk contrasts with the felt.

2 On each felt rectangle draw a horizontal line ½ inch (1.25 cm) down from the top with tailor's chalk.

▲ Make a chalk mark ¾ inch (2 cm) in from either side.

3 Now measure along the line, ¾ inch (2 cm) in from either side. Make a mark with chalk.

Put on a show!

▲ Cut diagonally to the nearest chalk mark.

4 Cut diagonally from one corner of the felt to the nearest chalk mark. Repeat on the other side and on both pieces.

5 Cut across the center line between the ears. That's better, now you can see the basic cat shape!

▲ A couple of backstitches make a perfect mouth for your cat.

6 On one of the cat-shaped pieces of felt, use a sewing needle and thread to sew on small buttons for the cat's eyes. Use tailor's chalk to draw in the nose and mouth. Using embroidery thread, sew two small overcast stitches in the center and a few backstitches either side for the mouth, following your chalk lines.

7 Cut a strip of the leftover felt, or a short length of yarn, to make the cat's tail. Position the tail at the bottom side edge of the other piece of cat-shaped felt (the back pattern). Overcast with the sewing thread.

▲ Try to keep your running stitch small and tidy.

8 Place the front cat piece on top of the back piece. Use the embroidery thread and a small running stitch to sew the two pieces together, close to the edge, leaving the bottom edge open.

Making the mouse

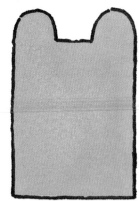

▲ The mouse shape should have more rounded ears than the cat.

1 Repeat steps 1–5 of Making the Cat, using the mouse-colored felt, but cut a more rounded shape for the ears.

2 Sew on two tiny beads for the eyes and embroider a small nose and mouth, as you did in step 6 of the cat puppet.

▲ You only need three large embroidery stitches to make some whiskers.

3 Sew three large stitches of embroidery thread on each side of the nose, for the whiskers.

4 Sew the two felt pieces together as you did in step 8 of the cat puppet.

Finger puppet people

Making the puppet people

▲ Make sure the face is the right size to fit onto the puppet.

1 For each of the three puppets, cut out two 2½ x 2 inch (6 x 5 cm) pieces of felt. Round off the top edge on all pieces.

2 For each face, use tailor's chalk to draw around a coin or spool of thread, marking a circle on the contrasting felt—remember the circle must fit onto the body felt piece. Cut out each felt circle.

▲ Use backstitch for the baby's eyes and mouth. You can also use this stitch for the boy and girl's mouths.

3 Sew on buttons or beads as eyes for the girl and boy. For the baby, use backstitch to sew sleepy eyes. Using embroidery thread, sew one small stitch in the middle of the face for the boy, girl and baby's noses.

▲ Try to keep your running stitch neat and tidy even though you are sewing around a circle!

4 Use a small running stitch to sew each face piece onto its body piece.

▲ Decorate your puppets with strands of yarn and beads for the hair.

5 Now you can get really creative and embellish your puppets with other decorations. You can use a few strands of yarn, about 2 inches (5 cm) long, as the boy's hair, and overcast them in the middle at the top of the head. Sew on beads for the girl's hair and decorate the puppets' bodies with buttons and bows.

6 Finally, sew the front pieces to the back pieces using running stitch, as you did with the cat and mouse puppets.

Materials

- Three 6 inch (15 cm) squares of felt, a different color for each person
- One 6 inch (15 cm) square of felt in a contrasting color to the first felt pieces, for the faces
- Decorations: buttons; beads; scraps of yarn; ribbon
- Sewing thread to match the buttons and beads
- Embroidery thread in various contrasting colors to the felt
- Sewing needle and emboidery needle
- Scissors
- Tape measure, tailor's chalk

With puppets on, kneel behind a table or box and entertain your family and friends with stories you have made up!

Stuffing

There are several different types of stuffing for toys. Synthetic batting is most often used. It can be bought by the yard or meter in various thicknesses, and is easily cut with scissors.

Foam is another type of stuffing and it can be bought in any shape and cut to size. It is available as chipped foam, bought in bags.

You can also easily make your own stuffing by cutting up scraps of fabric, yarn, or old clean clothes into small pieces. Keep them mixed up in a bag until you need to use some.

A round-headed tool, such as a large knitting needle, is useful for pushing the stuffing into small spaces.

Before you start the projects, practice by making and stuffing a small cushion.

1 Cut two squares of fabric approximately 6 x 6 inches (15 x 15 cm) and, with right sides together, pin and baste round the edge leaving a 2 inch (5 cm) gap in the middle of one side seam. Sew around the edge with a small running stitch. Remove the basting.

2 Now turn your cushion right side out.

3 Using small pieces of stuffing, gradually fill your cushion until it becomes quite firm. Push the stuffing down into the corners well.

4 Turn in the edges of the opening and overcast along the edge. Finish off at the top edge.

When you have this technique all sewn up, you can use it in the next project!

Tomato pin cushion

This plump, ripe tomato is ideal for keeping those pins neat. With its wobbly eyes and big embroidered grin, it also makes a good sewing companion.

Of course you can also use different colored felt to make other fruits or vegetables, such as orange for a happy tangerine pin cushion, or purple or beige for an unhappy onion, with a teardrop and sad mouth.

> This project only uses the skills you have learned so far, but if you have forgotten any, go back to the techniques pages to remind yourself.

Jolly juicy!

Materials

- One 11 inch (28 cm) square of red felt
- One 9 inch (23 cm) square of green felt
- Decorations: green ribbon; 2 toy eyes or buttons; small button or bead
- Sewing thread, green for the leaves and your choice of color for the decorations
- Embroidery thread, your choice of color for the face
- Strong thread, any color will do
- Sewing needle

- Embroidery needle
- Large needle
- Scissors
- Tailor's chalk
- Tape measure
- Stuffing
- One 5 inch (13 cm) square of pattern paper or thin paper
- Fabric glue, if needed

Making the tomato

1 Cut out a circle of red felt, about 11 inches (28 cm) across. You could draw around a plate or bowl with tailor's chalk as a guide.

⚠ Don't forget to leave a gap when you sew around the edges.

2 Thread a large needle with strong thread and tie both ends together. About ¼ inch (6 mm) in from the edge, sew a small running stitch most of the way around the felt circle. Stop sewing about 2 inches (5 cm) away from the end to leave a gap.

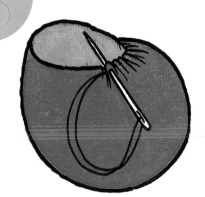

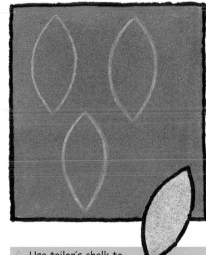

Making the top

1 Make a paper leaf pattern, about 3½ inches (9 cm) long and 2 inches (5 cm) across at the widest point.

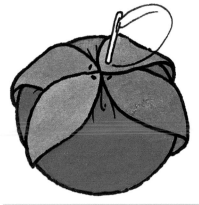

△ Stop the gathering from undoing with an overcast stitch.

3 Gently pull the thread to gather the top of the felt circle. When it is gathered up as much as possible, sew an overcast stitch to stop the gathering from undoing.

4 Fill the felt tomato with stuffing until it is quite firm and round.

△ Use tailor's chalk to draw around your paper leaf pattern on the green felt.

2 Cut out four leaf shapes from the green felt.

△ Place your leaves evenly around the top over the gathering and overcast onto the tomato one at a time.

3 Place one end of the first leaf over the gathered tomato top. Use a sewing needle and sewing thread to overcast the first leaf onto the tomato. Repeat for all four leaves, spacing them evenly around the top of the tomato.

4 Overcast a green ribbon loop on top of the leaves. Use fabric glue to stick on wobbly eyes or sew on button eyes. Sew on a small button or bead nose.

△ Pull gently to close up the tomato and finish off securely.

5 Sew around the rest of the top edge with a small running stitch and pull to close the hole, pushing the stuffing in as you go. Finish off securely.

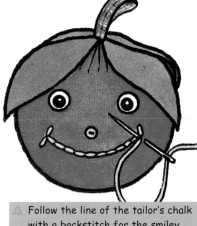

△ Follow the line of the tailor's chalk with a backstitch for the smiley mouth.

5 Draw a smiley mouth with tailor's chalk and backstitch with embroidery thread along the line.

Jolly juicy!

42

Your happy tomato is now ready to look after all your pins for you.

Drawstring

A drawstring is a cord, ribbon, elastic, or twill tape that is threaded through a hem—also known as a casing—such as at the mouth of a bag, and pulled tight to close it.

If you are using elastic that is shorter than the casing, pin one end of the elastic near the opening of the casing with a safety pin, then thread in the same way as with cord or ribbon. This will stop you from losing the end in the casing.

1 Measure 2 inches (5 cm) down from the top of the fabric. Mark with tailor's chalk across the whole piece of fabric. This is the fold line for your casing.

2 Fold along the line, pin, and baste. Remove the pins and use a small backstitch or sewing machine to stitch the seam close to its edge. Remove the basting.

4 When using cord, bind the end with tape, because it often frays. Thread a safety pin through cord or ribbon or, if you are using very thin cord, ribbon, or elastic, tie it through the safety pin securely.

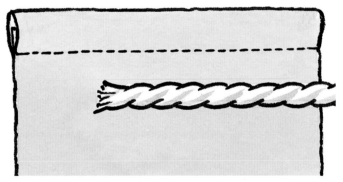

3 The drawstring must be slightly thinner than the casing to allow for easy threading and movement. For a 2 inch (5 cm) casing a 1½ inch (3.75 cm) drawstring is ideal. Use extra length and cut off later.

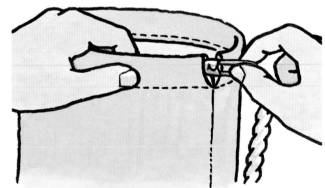

5 Thread the safety pin and drawstring through the casing at one end and ease it along gradually with both hands, until you get to the opening at the other end.

6 Carefully pull the cord through, remove the safety pin, and tie (or sew) the two ends of cord together.

Fabric pens

Fabric pens are great fun. You can use them to decorate bags, plain T-shirts, dolls' clothes, socks, fabric shoes, hats, or just about anything else that can be ironed. There is a wide range of fabric pens available at craft and sewing stores, including ones that are glossy, puffy, and glittery.

Remember to tell an adult when you use the iron. They may want to supervise, or you could ask an adult to do the pressing for you.

1 When using fabric pens on double-layered fabrics, such as items of clothing or bags, it is best to slide a piece of cardboard between the two layers, to keep the drawing from going through to the other side. Cut a piece of cardboard to fit snuggly inside the garment or bag.

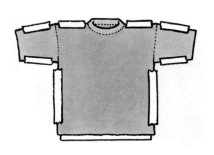 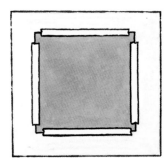

2 Attach the fabric and cardboard to a flat surface, or to another large piece of cardboard, using masking tape, to keep the garment from moving while you work.

3 Now follow the instructions on the pens to add your own designs to the fabric. Feel free to go wild, but, when using two or more colors, allow each color to dry before starting on the next, to ensure they don't run together. When drawing on knit or stretch fabric, be careful not to stretch it too much.

4 Leave the finished design to dry completely, then remove the masking tape and the cardboard from inside the garment.

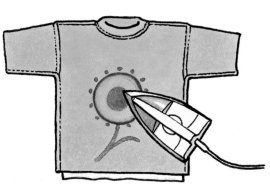

5 Turn the T-shirt wrong side out. Place a clean cloth between the layers, or underneath the fabric, and press on the reverse side. Check the pen instructions and the washing instructions on your fabric for temperature settings—you will probably need to use a medium to hot setting. Keep the iron moving slowly for a few minutes.

Tip

Light colors will not show up on dark fabrics, unless you use the glossy or puffy pens.

Designer drawstring bag

Drawstring bags are so useful, and can be easily made in various sizes. Large bags are great for laundry, sneakers, pajamas, or belts and scarves, and will keep any room neat. Hanging them on pegs in your bedroom will also show off your fantastic decorations. A small drawstring bag is very useful too, for jewelry, knik-knaks, makeup, toiletries, or secret treasures.

Look at the pictures and instructions on the techniques pages if you need to be reminded of any of the skills we have covered so far.

Making the bag

▲ Mark the fold line with tailor's chalk across the whole of the fabric.

1 Lay the medium-weight cotton fabric wrong side up on a flat surface. Measure 1½ inches (3.75 cm) down from the top edge. Mark with tailor's chalk across the whole piece of fabric. This is the fold line for your casing.

2 Turn the fabric over so it is now right side up. Fold it in half across the width. You will now be able to see half of the chalk line marked in the previous step.

The "wrong side" of the fabric is the side that you won't see when the garment or bag is finished. The "right side" is therefore the side of the fabric you will see when the sewing is finished. We often talk about laying the fabric "wrong side up" or "right side up," when the "wrong" or "right" side should be facing you.

Materials

- About 28 x 18½ inches (71 x 47 cm) medium-weight cotton fabric, in a light color
- About 48 inches (122 cm) of cord, or 2 inch (5 cm) wide twill tape or ribbon
- Decorations: felt; buttons; a bobble
- Sewing thread, to match the main fabric
- Sewing needle
- Scissors
- Pins
- Fabric pens
- Tape measure
- Tailor's chalk
- Cardboard
- Masking tape
- Cloth
- Iron with various settings
- Safety pin

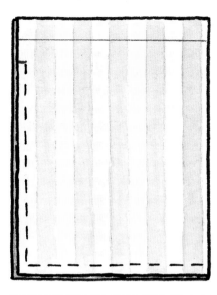

▲ Baste along the pin line and remove the pins.

3 Measure 3 inches (7.5 cm) down from the top edge (where the two sides meet) and mark with tailor's chalk. From this chalk mark, measure ½ inch (1.25 cm) in from the loose edges and pin all down the side and across the bottom edge. Baste along the pin line.

4 Remove the pins and sew the seams along the basting line using a small backstitch, then remove the basting.

5 Turn the bag right side out, pushing the corners out well.

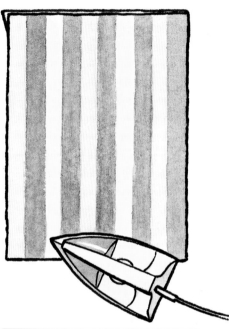

▲ Carefully press along the side seam and the bottom edge.

6 Make sure the seam is straight down one side and along the bottom and press.

Get creative with fabric pens and draw any design you like on your bag.

Decorating the bag

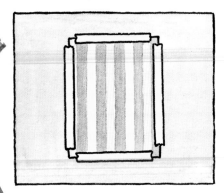

▲ Use masking tape to fix the bag and the cardboard to a flat surface.

1 Slide a piece of cardboard inside the bag and tape the bag to a flat surface.

▲ Use tailor's chalk to draw your design at first so you can correct any mistakes.

2 Lightly draw your design onto the bag with tailor's chalk.

▲ When you are happy with the design, draw around it carefully with a fabric pen.

3 Use a fabric pen to draw around the outline of the design. Allow it to dry before adding other colors. When the design is finished, let it dry thoroughly before removing the masking tape and cardboard.

▲ Remember to turn the bag wrong side out and keep the iron moving slowly.

4 Turn the bag wrong side out with the decorated side on top. Place a clean cotton cloth inside the bag and iron over the back of the drawing on a medium to hot setting for a few minutes.

5 Turn the bag right side out. Cut two small circles of felt and place a button on each. Sew through the buttons, felt, and front of the bag for each eye, then sew on a bobble nose.

Finishing the bag

▲ Stop sewing when you reach the chalk line.

1 Sew the remaining seam allowance to the inside of the bag.

▲ Fold the top edge to the inside of your bag along the chalk line and baste along the bottom edge.

2 Fold down the top edge to the inside of your bag along the chalk guideline. Fold a ½ inch (1.25 cm) hem under, along the bottom edge. Pin and baste round. Sew near the edge of the hem. Remove basting and gently press the casing.

3 Thread your cord through the casing, then tie the two ends together below the taped ends. Cut off the tape and fluff up the cord. Pull the cord to gather the top of your bag.

Now pack the bag and draw the cord to keep the contents secure. Why not embroider your initials on it and use it to take your gym clothes to school?

Customizing

There are so many cool things you can do to revamp your wardrobe. Some worn-out jeans can be revived with patches or made into a skirt. Simply changing the buttons will brighten up a dull blouse or skirt, while dyeing clothes will make faded garments look brand new. Cutting up T-shirts and adding ribbons, pockets, numbers, and drawings are other interesting options. So don't you dare throw anything away!

Revamping old sweaters

Cut off the sleeves of one old sweater, and sew on the sleeves from another, using different colors if possible. Attach the sleeves with blanket stitch, using an embroidery needle and a contrasting color of yarn.

Making jeans into a skirt

1 To make an old pair of jeans into a trendy skirt, first cut the legs off at your desired length. There is no need to hem the denim as it looks good cut and doesn't fray too much. You can trim any loose threads off. Cut the inside leg seams open, then cut up the center front seam to approximately ½ inch (1.25 cm) under the zipper.

2 Cut up the back center seam along the curved part approximately 2 inches (5 cm). Overlap the cut seam and sew together. Repeat down the front seam.

3 Lay your jeans on a flat surface and fit a piece of denim or other fabric (hem your fabric if it's not denim) in the gap between the front legs. Pin, baste, and sew in place. Trim off any excess on the inside. Turn your jeans over and repeat this between the back legs.

Make a cute tank top

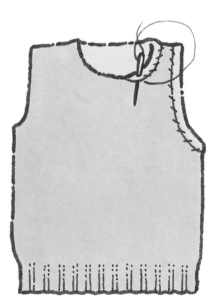

1 Cut off the sleeves around the seams of an old sweater. Cut the ribbing off the neck slightly lower at the front.

2 Turn a small hem (toward the outside) and overcast around the cut edges. Take care not to stretch the edges too much.

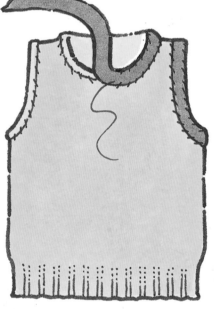

3 First pin, baste, and sew colored tape along the top edge around the neckline and armholes using a small overcast stitch. Turn in a small hem at the end of the tape and overlap to cover the other end, pin, baste. Ease the tape along the outside edge, covering your sewn hem. Pin, baste, and sew using a small overcast stitch. Sew over the end.

Techniques

Dyeing

Dye an old white blouse or shirt a bright color, referring to the instructions on the packet. Then replace the buttons with interesting new ones.

Cozy coat or jacket

Add a fur collar and cuffs to a plain coat or jacket and get cozy for the winter. Overcast the fur trim around the edges onto your garment.

Dressing up a plain tote bag

1 Cut off the old handle or handles close to the bag, and replace them with something more exciting! Make your own handles by braiding strands of yarn, ribbon, thin strips of denim, or use some decorative braid.

2 Measure the length of the handles or handle you need, turn in a small hem on both ends, pin and baste in place on the inside of the bag. Use an overcast stitch to sew in position.

3 Decorate the front of your bag with sequins, buttons, beads, or an interesting motif. Some motifs are iron-on. If you are using an iron-on motif, place a towel flat inside your bag, under your motif. Place a pressing cloth (a piece of cotton fabric) over your motif then, using a medium hot iron setting, iron over your motif for a few minutes until bonded to the fabric.

With these techniques at your fingertips, you have a cheap and chic way to make a new closet!

Hems and hemming

Hems should be as inconspicuous as possible and range from 1½ inches (3.75 cm) to 3 inches (7.5 cm) in depth. A hem neatens and strengthens a wide range of edges. There are a number of different ways to make a hem.

Tip

For thin or sheer fabrics, turn a narrow hem under twice and slipstitch or machine stitch along the hem.

Machine sewn hems

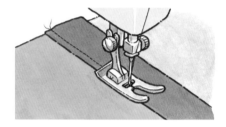

Hems can be machine sewn unless invisible stitching is needed. To machine stitch a hem, turn up the hem in the same way as above and sew along close to the turned edge, on the wrong side of the fabric.

Hemming tricky shapes

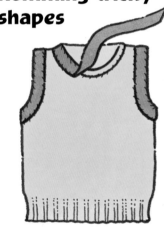

To hem around customized garments, a small hem can be folded outside the garment and a decorative tape sewn over the hem.

Hand sewn hems

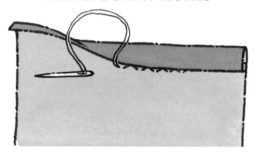

For lightweight fabrics, turn under the raw edge, about ¾ inch (2 cm), turn up the hem allowance, then baste along the hem ½ inch (1.25 cm) down from the folded top edge. To slipstitch the hem into place, pick up a small stitch on the garment, bring the needle out and sew through the hem.

Hems on a pocket

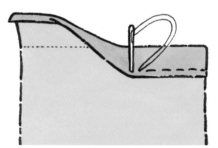

1 To make a simple pocket, measure the required size to fit on your garment, add a ½ inch (1.25 cm) seam allowance at the sides and the bottom edge. Add a 1 inch (2.5 cm) hem allowance for the top edge. Fold the top edge in twice, pin, baste, and sew along the folded edge.

2 Fold in the seam allowance down both sides and along the bottom edge, pin, and baste.

3 Position your pocket on your garment, pin, and baste onto your garment. Sew down the sides and across the bottom edge. Remove all basting.

T-shirt chic

It's so easy to add a bit of style to plain T-shirts. You can make dramatic changes with just a few scraps of fabric and some beads or ribbon.

Don't forget, you can look back to the techniques pages whenever you need help with any of the skills used for this project.

Native American style

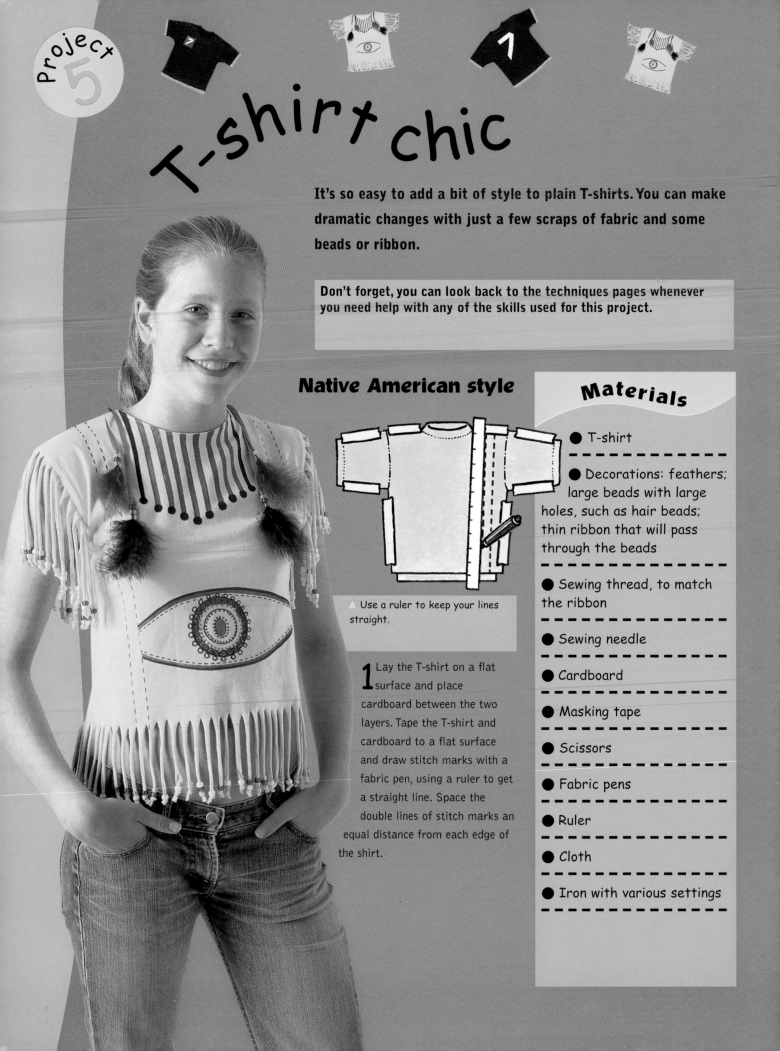

△ Use a ruler to keep your lines straight.

1 Lay the T-shirt on a flat surface and place cardboard between the two layers. Tape the T-shirt and cardboard to a flat surface and draw stitch marks with a fabric pen, using a ruler to get a straight line. Space the double lines of stitch marks an equal distance from each edge of the shirt.

Materials

● T-shirt

● Decorations: feathers; large beads with large holes, such as hair beads; thin ribbon that will pass through the beads

● Sewing thread, to match the ribbon

● Sewing needle

● Cardboard

● Masking tape

● Scissors

● Fabric pens

● Ruler

● Cloth

● Iron with various settings

2 Draw on more decoration, using the pictures on this page as a guide. You can draw around a cup or other round object as a guide for the center of the motif. Make sure each different color of fabric pen is dry before moving on to the next.

3 When you are happy with the design, leave it to dry completely. Remove the tape and cardboard and press the design on the reverse, with a cloth between the fabric layers.

Remember to tell an adult when you use the iron. They may want to supervise, or you could ask an adult to do the pressing for you.

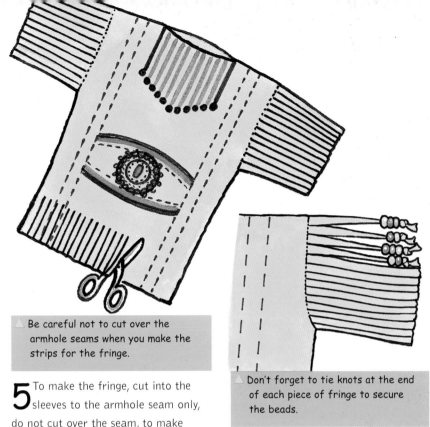

⚠ Be careful not to cut over the armhole seams when you make the strips for the fringe.

5 To make the fringe, cut into the sleeves to the armhole seam only, do not cut over the seam, to make roughly ⅜ inch (1 cm) wide strips. Cut a roughly 3½ inch (9 cm) long fringe along the bottom edge.

⚠ Don't forget to tie knots at the end of each piece of fringe to secure the beads.

6 Thread one or two large beads onto each piece of fringe and tie knots at the ends to secure them.

7 Use a few overcast stitches to sew feathers onto some thin ribbon. Thread more beads onto the ribbons and secure them with a few stitches. Then use a couple of overcast stitches to attach the decorated ribbon to the shoulders of the T-shirt.

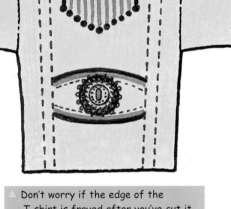

⚠ Don't worry if the edge of the T-shirt is frayed after you've cut it. This adds to the effect!

4 Cut off the neck ribbing and the hems on the sleeves and the bottom edge.

Sporty number

Materials

- T-shirt

- 2 yards (2 meters) striped braid, 1 inch (2.5 cm) wide

- 6 inches (15 cm) white cotton twill tape, 1/2 inch (1.25 cm) wide

- 15 inches (38 cm) white cotton twill tape, 1 inch (2.5 cm) wide

- 6 x 6 inches (15 x 15 cm) red cotton fabric

- Sewing thread, one to match the braid, red for the pocket, and white for the cotton tape

- Sewing needle

- Scissors

- Tailor's chalk

Try to keep your overcast stitch even and tidy as you sew around the hems and edge of the T-shirt.

1 Use a small overcast stitch to sew striped braid around the sleeve hems and bottom edge of the T-shirt.

2 Cut a patch of red cotton fabric 5½ inches (14 cm) long and 5 inches (13 cm) wide. Sew a small hem all around.

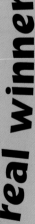

When you are happy with your number, pin, baste, and sew it to the pocket.

3 Fold the thin white cotton tape into a simple number seven shape. Pin the number to the center of the pocket. Baste, then remove the pins and sew with a small running stitch. Remove the basting.

If you have a sewing machine you can use it for the hemming and stitching (see page 22).

A real winner!

4 Position the pocket on the shirt and pin and baste in place, leaving the top edge open. Remove the pins and sew in place with a small running stitch, before removing the basting.

Use a running stitch to sew on your number seven as close to the edges as possible.

5 Draw a number seven on the back of the T-shirt with tailor's chalk. Fold the wider white cotton tape into a number seven and pin it to the back of the shirt, following your chalk guidelines. Baste to hold, then remove the pins before sewing on, close to the edges, and removing the basting.

There you have it! A collection of what look like brand new T-shirts. Now you can become a fashion designer and think up your own ways of customizing old clothes. Soon your family and friends will be asking you to jazz-up their worn-out gear.

Handmade buttonholes

There are several different types of buttonholes. Buttonholes are worked on the right side of the garment for girls and on the left side for boys. Horizontal buttonholes are used for most garments, especially on waistbands and thicker fabrics. Shirts and blouses have vertical buttonholes as the buttonholes take up less width. The buttons are usually small and fit snuggly into the buttonhole. For thin fabrics use double fabric or iron-on interfacing (see page 91).

> Hand-worked buttonholes are made after the garment is finished and buttonhole stitch (or blanket stitch) is used to sew around the edges of a buttonhole.

Horizontal buttonhole

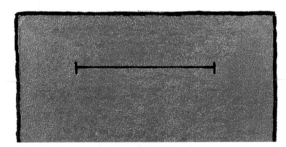

1 First measure the button across the center. Using tailor's chalk, draw a straight, horizontal line, the same length as the button, on the fabric in the chosen position.

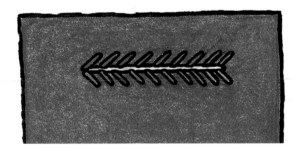

2 Cut along the chalk line carefully with sharp pointed scissors. Overcast, with double sewing thread, along the cut edges of the buttonhole. This stops any stretching while sewing.

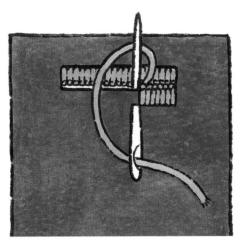

3 Start at the back of your fabric and sew a close blanket stitch around the edges.

Tip

Practice a large and small buttonhole on a spare piece of cloth!

● ● ● ● ● ● ● ● ● ● ● ● ● ● ● ● ● ● ●

Making a button shank

When a button goes through a buttonhole, it needs a shank. To make a shank, use the same sewing technique as for any button, but use longer stitches, so there is space between the button and the fabric. Wind the thread around the stitches a few times and add a backstitch. Then finish off in the usual way.

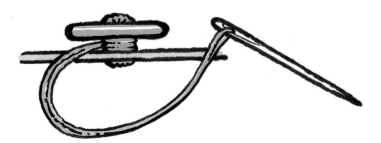

Vertical buttonhole

1 Measure the button across the center, then draw a straight, vertical line, the same length as the button, on the fabric in the chosen position.

2 Cut along the line to make the buttonhole and overcast the cut edges as with the horizontal buttonhole.

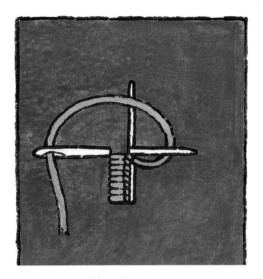

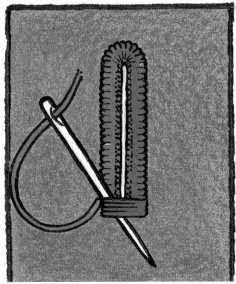

3 Buttonholes for front fastenings are sewn in the same way, adding a bar tack at either end. A bar tack is a few overcast stitches at the end of the buttonhole, reaching over both sides of the buttonhole. This strengthens the ends.

Denim cushion cover

Buttons and buttonholes are not only used on clothes. In this project the button neatly closes up a cushion cover. Making this cushion cover is a great way to use up worn-out jeans or ones that have become too small. But don't forget to ask the owner if they are not yours.

This project uses buttonhole stitch and some of the stitching and embroidery skills you have already learned. But don't worry if you have forgotten anything, simply flip back to any of the techniques pages for a quick reminder.

Materials

● Pair of old jeans
- - - - - - - - - - - - - - -
● Cotton fabric, any color for the inner cushion, enough for two cushions
- - - - - - - - - - - - - - -
● Two large buttons
- - - - - - - - - - - - - - -
● Yarn, brightly colored
- - - - - - - - - - - - - - -
● Sewing thread for basting
- - - - - - - - - - - - - - -
● Sewing needle for basting
- - - - - - - - - - - - - - -
● Large needle
- - - - - - - - - - - - - - -
● Scissors and pins
- - - - - - - - - - - - - - -
● Stuffing, enough for two cushions
- - - - - - - - - - - - - - -
● Motifs for decoration
- - - - - - - - - - - - - - -

Preparing the pieces

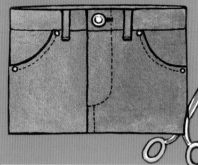

▲ Cut down the side seams of the shortened jeans to make a separate back and front.

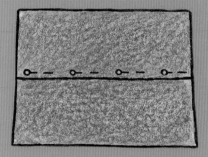

▲ Pin together the top and bottom leg pieces where they overlap.

1 Cut off the legs of the jeans at the crotch, then cut down the side seams. You will now have a separate back and front. You are going to use the back, with the pockets, to make the front panel of the cushion cover.

2 Use a leg piece to make the back panel of the cover. First cut along the seams of one leg. You will now have two leg pieces. On a flat surface, lay the leg pieces next to each other, horizontally. Now overlap the top leg piece 1½ inches (3.75 cm) on top of the bottom piece. Pin together.

3 Pin the front panel of the cover onto the overlapped leg pieces. Cut the leg pieces to the same size as the front panel, then unpin and remove the front panel again.

Blanket stitching the overlap edges

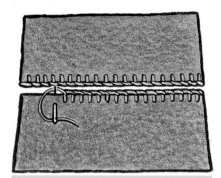

▲ Use a bright color to blanket stitch along the edges.

1 Unpin the overlapped back panel. Use brightly colored yarn and a large needle to blanket stitch along the edges that were overlapping.

2 Overlap the back panel again, then pin and baste in place. Remove the pins.

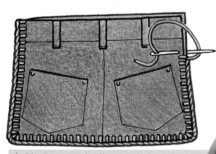

▲ Blanket stitch all around the edges to make the basic cushion cover.

3 Pin the back and front panels together and baste. Remove the pins and use the yarn to blanket stitch all around the cushion cover. Remove the basting. Now you have the basic cushion cover.

Making the buttonhole

1 Find the center of the back overlapped panel and mark it with tailor's chalk. Remove the basting stitches.

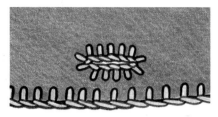

▲ You don't need a tightly closed buttonhole stitch for this buttonhole.

Making the inner cushion

1 Cut a square the same size as the denim cover from two layers of cotton fabric.

2 Sew the two pieces together around the edges, but leave a 3½ inch (9 cm) gap at the top.

2 Measure the button and draw a line on the denim for the buttonhole. Cut the slit, overcast the edges with sewing thread, then buttonhole stitch with the yarn.

3 Use tailor's chalk to mark through the middle of the buttonhole onto the denim underneath the overlap.

4 Sew the button to the panel underneath using the yarn and adding a shank.

▲ Remember to leave a gap to push your stuffing into.

3 Now push some stuffing through the gap and sew it up. Simple!

Now just push the inner cushion into the denim cover and button the button.

Why not make a second cover with the remaining front piece and legs of the jeans? Add decoration by sewing on butterfly and flower motifs, or embroidering your initials, before you add the stuffing of course!

Using elastic

Elastic stretches and shrinks, to a certain degree, to fit the person wearing it, so it is often used in waistbands and cuffs. There are a few different kinds of elastic. Wide elastic is what you need for waistbands and cuffs, while thin elastic is used in narrow hems of garments made from fine fabric, to gather the edges of sleeves, necks, and waists.

To practice using elastic you can make a hem at the edge of some scrap fabric. As you do this, imagine that the hem is at the waist of a skirt.

Cutting wide elastic for waistbands

Measure your waist, as shown on page 17, and cut the wide elastic so that it is 1 inch (2.5 cm) shorter than the measurement. This also allows for a ¾ inch (2 cm) overlap to sew the ends together. Other measurements do not need to be as fitted.

Cutting wide elastic for cuffs

For cuffs, measure around your wrist and cut the wide elastic to the same length. This still allows for a ¾ inch (2 cm) overlap to sew the ends together.

Using wide elastic

1 Make a casing that is wide enough to thread the elastic through. Use a safety pin to pin one end of the elastic to the fabric near the casing opening—this stops the elastic from disappearing into the casing when you thread the other end through. Attach the other end of the elastic to another safety pin and thread this through the casing.

2 Push the elastic all the way through the casing by scrunching up the fabric from the outside. When the safety pin comes out at the other end, remove both safety pins, and pull out the ends of the elastic.

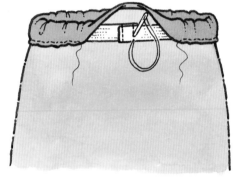

3 Overlap the ends of the elastic by about ¾ inch (2 cm). Pin the overlapping ends together and baste. Then remove the pins and sew the ends together.

4 Pull the casing over to cover the elastic and sew up the gap in the casing.

Tip

When using wide elastic try not to twist it as you pull it through your casing.

Using thin elastic

1 Make a casing that is wide enough to thread the elastic through. Use a small safety pin to pin one end of the elastic to the fabric near the casing opening, as before. Tie the other end of the elastic to another small safety pin and thread this through the casing.

2 Push the elastic all the way through the casing by scrunching up the fabric from the outside. When the safety pin comes out at the other end, remove both safety pins, and pull out the ends of the elastic.

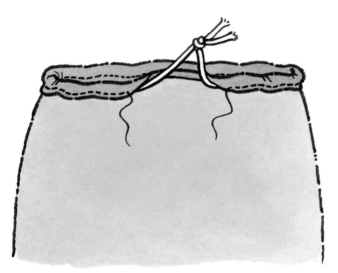

3 Tie the two ends together in a secure knot and trim off the ends of the elastic. Pull the casing over to cover the elastic and sew up the gap in the casing.

Using shirring elastic

Shirring elastic is used for ruching— gathering—fabric while keeping it stretchy. It is often used around sleeve edges and waists, or all over on thin fabrics. Shirring elastic is threaded onto a needle and sewn in a running stitch, like thread.

1 Shirring elastic is usually sewn in even lines around the edges or across the front of a garment before constructing the garment. You will need to allow an extra 2–6 inches (5–15 cm) on the width of the pattern for gathering, so remember this when you cut out your fabric.

2 Use tailor's chalk and a ruler to draw guidelines on the fabric. You can draw one line or many, about ½ inch (1.25 cm) apart.

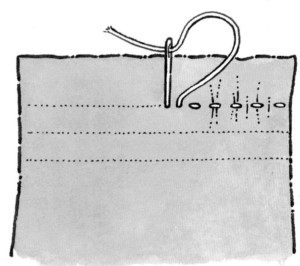

3 Thread a single thread of shirring elastic onto a large needle and tie a knot at the end. Sew a running stitch along the lines and pull gently to gather, not too tight! Finish off each line as usual.

Now you can try out the project on the next page which uses this technique and others you have learned!

Two skirts in one

This is a simple but gorgeous reversible skirt that is suitable for any occasion. If you have access to a sewing machine you'll be able to zip this out in no time. If not, don't worry, it is still super-easy to sew by hand. You can decorate the front with any colorful ribbon, cord, or braid. Why not make one for your best friend too?

This project only uses the skills you have learned so far, but if you have forgotten any, go back to the techniques pages to remind yourself.

Materials

- ½ yard (0.5 m) lightweight denim, 45 inches (1.15 m) wide

- ½ yard (0.5 m) lightweight floral fabric, 45 inches (1.15 m) wide

- ¾ inch (2 cm) wide elastic, enough to fit around your waist without stretching

- Decorations: cord or ribbon in two different colors; iron-on motif

- Sewing thread to match the fabrics

- Sewing needle

- Sewing machine (optional)

- Scissors and pins

- Large safety pin

- Iron with various settings

- Tape measure and ruler

- Tailor's chalk

Inside out fashion!

Cutting the skirt patterns

1 First wash separately, then press, the main fabrics.

> **Remember to tell an adult when you use the iron. They may want to supervise, or you could ask an adult to do the pressing for you.**

2 Measure around the widest part of your hips and add 5 inches (13 cm). This will be the width of fabric. Measure the desired length of your skirt, adding 1¾ inches (4.5 cm) for hem allowances. Cut out both the denim and floral fabrics to these measurements, cutting close to the edges of the fabric to leave extra material for making pockets.

Making pockets

1 Cut two pocket shapes (one from each of the leftover main fabrics), 6 inches x 5½ inches (15 cm x 14 cm).

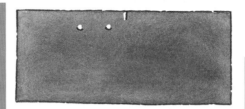

> Use tailor's chalk to mark where the top edge of the pockets will be positioned.

2 Make a chalk mark at the center point along the top edge of each skirt piece, on the right side of the fabric. Measure 3 inches (7.5 cm) to the left and 3 inches (7.5 cm) down from this center point and mark with chalk. From this chalk mark, measure a straight line 4½ inches (11.5 cm) to the left and mark with chalk. Repeat on the second skirt piece. You will use these new marks to align the top edge of each pocket.

> After you have removed the pins, sew along the folded hem with a small running stitch.

3 Turn down the top edge of each pocket, first ½ inch (1.25 cm) then another ½ inch (1.25 cm) toward the wrong side of the fabric. Pin, baste, remove the pins, and sew across the hem. Remove the basting.

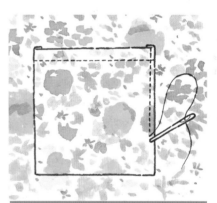

> Sew on the pocket using a neat running stitch.

4 Turn in ½ inch (1.25 cm) to the wrong side of the fabric around the three remaining edges. Pin, baste, and remove the pins. Press the pockets. Position the top of each pocket between the chalk marks on the skirt piece and pin and baste in place. Sew close to the pocket edges, leaving the top edge open.

Making the skirt

1 Place one piece of skirt fabric on top of the other with the right sides together. Leave a ½ inch (1.25 cm) seam allowance from the top edge, and pin, then baste the fabrics together.

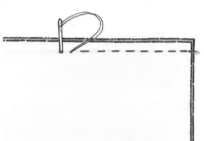

▲ Use a small running stitch to sew along the basting line at the top edge.

2 Remove the pins and sew along the basting line, either by hand using a small running stitch, or on a sewing machine. Remove the basting.

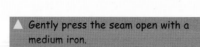

▲ Gently press the seam open with a medium iron.

3 Open the seam and carefully press it flat.

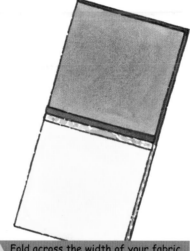

▲ Fold across the width of your fabric, matching the seams at the edge.

4 Fold across the width of your joined together fabric, right sides together. Lay your fabric flat with the seam going across the middle.

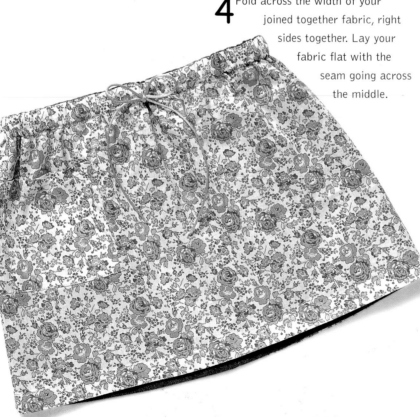

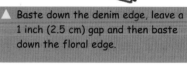

▲ Baste down the denim edge, leave a 1 inch (2.5 cm) gap and then baste down the floral edge.

5 Pin the side edge leaving a ¾ inch (2 cm) seam allowance. Starting on the denim fabric, baste to the middle seam. Leave a 1 inch (2.5 cm) gap, then baste down the rest of the edge. Remove pins. Sew by hand or machine stitch. Remove the basting and press the seam open.

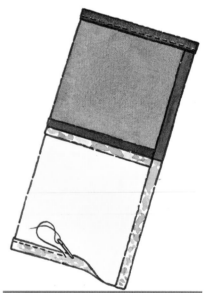

▲ Make a hem all around the edge of both ends.

6 Hem both ends by turning over a ½ inch (1.25 cm) then ¾ inch (2 cm) hem, toward the wrong side of the fabric. Pin and baste the hem edges, remove the pins and hand or machine stitch close to the edge. Remove the basting.

▲ To create the finished skirt shape, pull the denim fabric half down over the floral fabric half.

7 Fold the denim half down so that the wrong sides of the fabrics are together. You now have a tube with one fabric on the inside and the other facing out. Press along the top edge. Well done. Now you can see what the finished skirt is going to look like.

8 To make the waistband casing to thread the elastic through, measure 1 inch (2.5 cm) down from the top edge. Pin, baste, and remove pins. Sew by hand or machine stitch all the way around and remove the basting.

9 Measure your waist and cut the elastic 1 inch (2.5 cm) shorter than the measurement. Find the gap left in the top of your side seam and thread the elastic through with a large safety pin.

10 Overlap the elastic and sew securely, then sew up the opening in the seam.

11 Decorate the finished skirt with a cord or ribbon bow on either side, and sew or iron on a motif on the denim side.

Congratulate yourself on making your first skirt, which is actually your first and second skirt in one!

Quilting

Quilting is the technique of joining three layers of fabric together to make a slightly squishy pad. To do this, you need a top layer, an interlining (filling), and a backing layer. You can make one large quilt, with stitching in patterns in between to keep the filling in place, or make small quilted panels to stitch together later.

Quilting materials

The fabric for the top and back layers of the quilt can be cotton, silk, satin, or lightweight wool. Colored or printed fabric makes a particularly effective backing. For the filling, batting gives a puffier effect than fleece and comes in different weights (thicknesses).

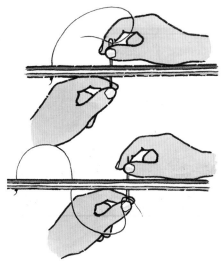

How to quilt

The traditional quilting stitch is a simple running stitch. These stitches are usually small, evenly spaced, and close together.

1 Lay the backing fabric on a flat surface, wrong side up, and place the filling on top. Then position the top layer, right side up, on top of the filling.

2 Pin and baste all around with sewing thread and a sewing needle, close to the edge. Remove the pins. This basting will keep the squares together while you stitch the quilting pattern.

3 Use tailor's chalk to draw a design on the top piece of fabric. To baste along the lines, through all three layers—to stop any movement between them—thread a single strand of sewing thread onto a sewing needle and make a knot at the end. Bring the needle through from the back to the top of the quilt. Hold your left hand under the quilt. At the next stitch position, use your right hand to push the needle straight down, not at an angle. Draw the needle and thread through with your left hand. Continue in this way over your design.

4 Thread your embroidery needle with a single strand of quilting thread or embroidery thread, then make a knot at one end. Start sewing from the center out toward the edge. This will keep the quilt even throughout. Hold the needle the same way as in step 3 and sew a small, even running stitch along your basting guidelines. Finish off. Remove basting when finished.

You can use any decorative patterns on your quilt, but remember to cover the quilt evenly to hold the three layers securely in place.

Binding

Binding is a neat way to finish off edges and add an interesting feature. You can use ribbon, decorative tape, bias binding, or strips of fabric. Make sure the binding material you choose is wide enough to fold over the edge of your fabric. Ribbon, tape, and strips of fabric are ideal to use for straight edges, whereas bias binding is used for both straight and curved edges.

Binding straight edges

1 Place half the binding material over the edge of the fabric you are practicing on. Pin, baste, and sew down one side using a small running stitch or working on a sewing machine.

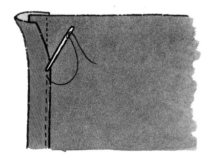

2 Fold the other edge of the binding material over the edge of your fabric and pin, baste, and sew as before.

Using bias binding

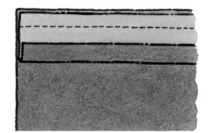

1 Bias binding has a hem on either side. Open up one hem, place the fold line of the binding to the seam allowance of the garment, right sides together (the edges tuck around to the wrong side) and pin, baste, and sew along the fold line of the bias binding.

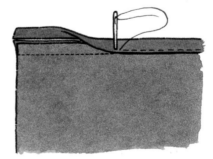

2 Trim off excess seam allowance to the raw edge of the binding. Fold the binding over the garment edge down to the stitched line, keep the hem on the outer edge tucked under, and slipstitch along the folded edge line.

Making your own binding

1 To make your own binding out of strips of fabric, cut enough width to cover the edge of the main fabric and add a small hem allowance on both sides. Sew the binding on in the same way as for straight binding, but tuck in hems on both sides to keep the binding material from fraying.

2 Cut strips of fabric on the bias for bias binding, sewing it on in the same way as bias binding.

Quilted Japanese bag

Make this beautiful quilted bag. It has interesting tassel and bead details and everyone will love the quilted sides! It has a useful shoulder strap and is the perfect accessory for any special occasion.

This project uses the sewing skills you have already learned, which by now are quite a few. If you need to be reminded of any of the techniques, simply look back at the illustrations and instructions on the techniques pages.

Materials

- ½ yard (0.5 m) satin fabric, 36 inches (1 m) wide
- ½ yard (0.5 m) backing fabric, 36 inches (1 m) wide
- ½ yard (0.5 m) medium-weight batting, 36 inches (1 m) wide
- 1½ yards (1.5 m) satin ribbon, 1 inch (2.5 cm) wide
- Sewing thread and needle
- Embroidery thread in a contrasting color to the fabrics

- Two tassels in a color of your choice
- Medium embroidery needle
- Sewing machine (optional)
- Scissors and pins
- Tailor's chalk
- Cardboard
- 2 medium beads
- Medium snap

Party time!

Quilting the sides of the bag

Wash separately, then press, your satin and backing fabric before cutting out squares.

1 Cut two 10 inch (25 cm) squares from each of the satin fabric, backing fabric, and batting.

2 Place the backing square on a flat surface, wrong side up. Put the batting square on top, with a satin square, right side up, on top of that.

3 Pin all three layers together 1 inch (2.5 cm) in from the edges. Baste with sewing thread and remove the pins.

When you are happy with your design, baste through all three layers with sewing thread.

4 Leaving a 1½ inch (3.75 cm) margin all around the edges, lightly draw a pattern in tailor's chalk on the top satin square. Use the sewing thread to baste along these lines through all three fabric layers, remembering to keep the needle straight as you push through the materials.

5 Starting from the center of the pattern, stitch over the basting using embroidery thread and a medium embroidery needle. Remove the basting.

Carefully trim off the excess fabric with scissors. The tailor's chalk can be brushed off easily.

6 Mark a 9 x 8 inch (23 x 20 cm) rectangle centrally around the quilting pattern with tailor's chalk. Baste through all three layers ½ inch (1.25 cm) inside the chalk line. Trim off the excess fabric outside the chalk mark.

7 Repeat steps 2–6 to make a second quilted panel.

Binding the top edges

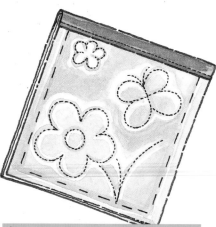

△ Fold the binding over and pin, baste, and sew as for the other side of the bag.

△ The edge of the bag should lie across the middle of the binding so that half of the binding folds over.

1 To bind the top edge of one panel with ribbon, start by pinning and basting the edge of the ribbon to the backing fabric. Sew the binding on with sewing thread and remove the basting.

2 Fold the binding over to cover the basting at the edge of the quilted panel. Pin, baste, and sew the binding, then remove all the pins and basting stitches. Bind the top edge of the second quilted panel in the same way.

Putting together the bag

△ Baste down the sides of the bag to hold the bag in place.

1 Position the two quilted panels together, with the linings facing each other and the top bound edges together, and pin and baste down the sides and along the bottom edge.

2 Bind the bottom edge with ribbon as before, and remove the basting.

3 To bind the sides, start at the bottom with one end of the remaining ribbon. Tuck in a small hem and bind up to the top edge, try not to twist the ribbon as you do so. Without cutting the ribbon, use the other end of the ribbon at the bottom of the other side of the bag and bind as before. The leftover ribbon that has not been used to bind the sides will become the bag's handle.

Party time!

Fill your bag with everything you need to take to the party!

Sew the ribbon handle in half neatly to finish off.

4 Sew the ribbon in half from where the binding ends on one side to where it begins on the other, to finish.

Finishing touches

Sew the bead in the same way as the beads on the fringe of the bejeweled belt project (page 32).

1 Sew a bead onto the top of each tassel and then sew each bead, with its tassel attached, onto each corner of the bag.

2 To finish, sew a snap in the middle of the top edge, on the inside of the bag.

No one else will have a bag like this, but I bet everyone will soon wish they had!

Appliqué

Appliqué is the technique of sewing small pieces of fabric, often cut into decorative shapes, onto a larger piece, either by hand or machine. It is a great way to use up scraps of fabric, especially since you can use any type of fabric.

Why not use appliqué to personalize plain garments, cushion covers, and towels for presents, or to decorate clothes, bags, and bed linen? Appliquéd wall hangings and pictures brighten up any room, or you could join small patches of appliqué to make a great quilt for your bed.

Look at page 13 for information on using a seam ripper and embroidery hoops.

Practicing zigzag stitch on a sewing machine

On a sewing machine, zigzag stitch is used to attach the appliqué motifs to the main fabric.

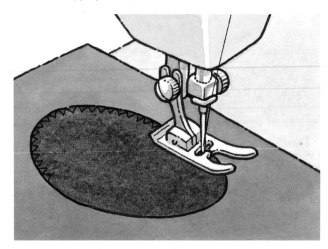

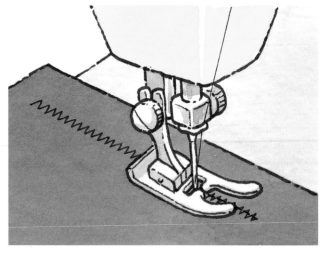

1 Set the sewing machine to close zigzag stitch. Follow the steps on page 22 to practice this stitch on a plain piece of fabric. Now practice again by sewing around another scrap of fabric to attach it.

2 Finish zigzag stitch by changing the setting to a straight stitch, with the needle out of the fabric, then reverse for a short distance and trim off the thread ends.

Cutting out appliqué pieces

1 Draw your own designs onto scraps of fabric no larger than 10 inches (25 cm) square. If you plan to machine stitch your designs with zigzag stitch you do not need to add a seam allowance, unless your fabric is loosely woven and frays a lot. For hand stitching, add a ¼ inch (6 mm) seam allowance all around the motif.

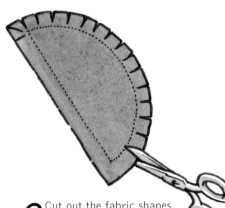

2 Cut out the fabric shapes. If you have a seam allowance, you can snip into it as shown. This helps reduce bulk when turning the fabric in.

3 Turn in the seam allowance and pin and baste close to the edges. When hemming awkward shapes a seam ripper helps to tuck in the edges. Remove the pins.

Sewing on the appliqué pieces

1 Position the appliqué pieces on the base fabric in a pattern of your choice. Pin and baste in place. If some designs are going to overlap, first work on the pieces that will be underneath, and gradually build up your design. Remove the pins and press well on the back of the base fabric to keep all the pieces very flat.

Remember to let an adult know when you want to use the iron. They may want to do the pressing for you, or supervise when you do it yourself.

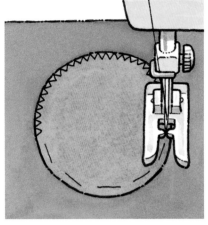

2 To stitch the pieces in place with a sewing machine, use a large zigzag stitch to sew all around the edges. Make sure the zigzag stitch is wide enough to completely cover the edges of the appliqué patch.

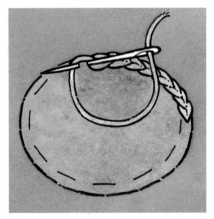

3 If you want to sew the patches on by hand, place the section of base fabric you are working on in an embroidery hoop and use any decorative embroidery stitch with single embroidery thread to sew around the edges.

You can make beautiful pictures from your appliqué work by folding the base fabric around a piece of cardboard and sticking down the edges on the reverse.

Day and night pillowcase

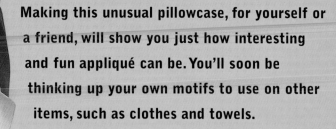

Making this unusual pillowcase, for yourself or a friend, will show you just how interesting and fun appliqué can be. You'll soon be thinking up your own motifs to use on other items, such as clothes and towels.

Don't forget that you can look back to the techniques pages whenever you need help with any of the skills used for this project.

Materials

- ³/₄ yard (68 cm) light blue cotton fabric, 36 inches (1 m) wide

- ³/₄ yard (68 cm) dark blue cotton fabric, 36 inches (1 m) wide

- ¹/₂ yard (0.5 m) yellow cotton fabric

- ¹/₂ yard (0.5 m) white cotton fabric

- ¹/₂ yard (0.5 m) pale pink cotton fabric

- Scissors and tape measure

- Pillow

- Tailor's chalk

- Pattern cutting paper and pencil

FOR MACHINE APPLIQUÉ

- Sewing machine

- Gold and silver soft lurex thread

- Sewing thread: light blue, dark blue, and white

FOR HAND APPLIQUÉ

- Thin gold and silver embroidery thread

- Thin white embroidery thread

- Orange embroidery thread

- Embroidery thread, your choice of color for the eye and mouth of the moon

- Sewing needle

- Embroidery needle

Sleepy head!

Cutting out the pillowcase

⚠ Transfer your measurements onto the light blue fabric and cut out the pillow pattern.

1 Measure the length and width of your pillow. Transfer these measurements to the light blue cotton fabric, adding ½ inch (1.25 cm) all around for the seam allowance. Draw the shape onto the right side of the fabric with tailor's chalk. Draw another chalk line, 2 inches (5 cm) away from the short end on the right side for a hem, leaving the original chalk line still visible. Cut out the pillow pattern.

⚠ Add an extra 8 inches (20 cm) to the dark blue fabric.

2 Follow step 1 with the dark blue cotton fabric, but this time add 8 inches (20 cm) to one short end, leaving the original chalk line still visible.

Arranging the appliqué motifs

1 Draw a bold sun, sunshine rays, and a cloud for the daytime side of the pillowcase on a piece of pattern cutting paper. You could draw around a small plate to make a good circle for the sun. Cut out the shapes.

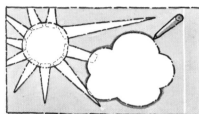

⚠ Arrange the paper sun and cloud on the pale blue fabric and draw around them with tailor's chalk.

2 Lay the pale blue piece of fabric on a flat surface so that the chalk line on the short end is on the right-hand side. Arrange the paper pattern pieces, leaving a 1½ inch (3.75 cm) margin around the edge of the cloud, inside the seam allowances. The sun should be on the left of the pillow.

3 Move the rays up so the sun overlaps the edges of the rays by about ¼ inch (6 mm). If any rays are underneath the cloud, mark the place where they overlap and trim off the excess ray, allowing a ¼ inch (6 mm) overlap. Pin the paper patterns in place and draw around them with tailor's chalk. Remove the pins.

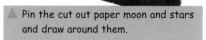

⚠ Pin the cut out paper moon and stars and draw around them.

4 For the nighttime side of the pillow, cut out a crescent moon and some stars from pattern paper. Lay the dark blue cotton fabric on a flat surface so that the chalk line on the short end is on the left-hand side this time. Position the moon on the right of the fabric, farthest from the short-end hem, with the stars in between. Pin and draw around the shapes before removing the pins.

5 If you are planning to sew by machine, pin the same paper shapes to the other pieces of colored cotton—yellow for the sun and rays, white for the cloud and moon, and pale pink for the stars. If you plan to sew by hand, draw around the paper motifs onto another piece of paper, then add a ¼ inch (6 mm) seam allowance around each piece. Cut these patterns out and pin them to the yellow, white, and pale pink fabrics. Draw around the shapes, remove the pins and carefully cut out the motifs.

Sewing on the appliqué: daytime

Lay the light blue cotton on a flat surface with the chalk hemline on the right.

By machine

1 Place the yellow rays in position within the chalk marks. Pin and baste well, then remove the pins.

⚠ Practice a large zigzag stitch on a piece of leftover fabric before you start on the real thing.

2 Thread the machine with gold soft lurex thread on top and light blue thread in the bobbin. Set the stitch to a large zigzag with close stitches. On some of the leftover cotton fabric, practice the machine stitch to ensure it covers the edges completely.

3 When you have found the right size stitch, start on the pillowcase at one end of one of the rays, and sew down to the point. Leave the needle in the fabric, lift the foot, and turn the fabric around so the other side of the ray is in position to sew. Sew along the other edge.

4 To finish off the zigzag, make sure the needle is out of the fabric, change the stitch setting to straight stitch, and sew back a few stitches. Then trim the thread.

5 Return to the original zigzag setting and sew on the remaining rays as before.

6 Iron the reverse of the fabric, then position the sun within the chalk lines. Remember it will overlap the rays slightly. Pin and baste, and machine stitch as before, zigzag stitching over the top of the rays.

7 Remove the gold thread and rethread with white. Place the cloud in position, pin, and baste. Remove the pins and sew around the edge with the same zigzag stitch. When everything is sewn on, iron the reverse of the fabric.

Remember to tell an adult when you use the iron. They may want to supervise, or you could ask an adult to do the pressing for you.

By hand

Follow the same order as machine sewing—rays, sun, cloud. Choose a decorative stitch. Don't forget to snip around curved edges and into corners.

1 Place the yellow rays in position within the chalk marks, remembering to turn in a ¼ inch (6 mm) hem. Pin and baste well, then remove the pins.

2 Using thin gold embroidery thread, embroider a line of stitching all around the first ray. Finish off then complete each ray in the same way.

3 Iron the reverse of the fabric, then turn in a ¼ inch (6 mm) hem all around the sun and pin it in place. Remember it will overlap the rays slightly. Baste and embroider as before, stitching over the top of the rays.

4 Place the cloud in position, not forgetting the hem, and pin and baste. Remove the pins and sew around the edge with thin white embroidery thread. When everything is sewn on, iron the reverse of the fabric.

Decoration

⚠ Draw on some features and embroider over the chalk lines.

Draw a smile, eyes, eyebrows, and a nose with chalk. Use orange embroidery thread and a running stitch to sew over them. For the pupils, make stitches starting at the center of the eye and splaying out in a star shape.

Sewing on the appliqué: nighttime

1 Lay the dark blue cotton on a flat surface. Place the stars and moon in position on the chalk marks, remembering to turn in ¼ inch (6 mm) when hand sewing, pin and baste. Remove the pins.

2 Follow the instructions in Machine or Hand Sewing to stitch the stars in place, using silver lurex thread on top and dark blue in the bobbin, or silver embroidery thread if working by hand.

3 Change the silver thread to white to sew on the moon. Draw on an eye and mouth and embroider with embroidery thread. Press well on the reverse.

Sleepy head!

Putting together the pillowcase

By machine

1 Change the stitching on your machine to a medium straight stitch. Thread the machine with light blue on top and in the bobbin.

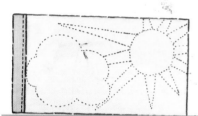

⚠ Baste down the line of the hem, then remove the basting after you've sewn along it.

2 On the daytime side, first turn under ½ inch (1.25 cm) then a 1½ inch (3.75 cm) hem along the chalkline to the wrong side. Pin and baste. Remove the pins and sew down the hem.

3 Rethread the machine with dark blue thread, on top and in the bobbin. On the edge of the nighttime side that has the chalk hemline, turn in a ½ inch (1.25 cm) hem, twice, toward the wrong side. Pin, baste, and remove the pins. Sew down the hem and remove the basting and press.

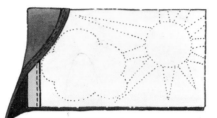

⚠ Cover the light blue hem by folding over the dark blue fabric.

4 Lay the dark blue side, right side up, on a flat surface. Lay the light blue side, wrong side up, on top with the unhemmed sides together. At the hemmed ends, fold the dark blue fabric over the light blue fabric along the edge of the light blue hem.

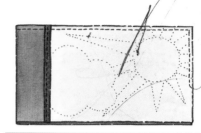

⚠ Leave the folded edge as it is but pin, baste, and sew around the rest of the edges.

5 Pin and baste the top and bottom edges and the side seam. Sew about ½ inch (1.25 cm) in from the edges, leaving the folded edge unsewn.

By hand

If you are sewing by hand, use light blue thread for the daytime side, dark blue for the nighttime side, and either color to sew the pillowcase together. Follow the instructions for sewing by machine, but use a medium sewing needle and a small running stitch where machine stitching is suggested.

Turn the pillowcase right sides out, tucking in the pillow flap, and press well. Put your pillow inside the case and flap over the end. Sleep well on the nighttime side and turn over to the daytime side to brighten your morning when you wake up.

Gathering

If you make a line of stitches and pull the thread, the fabric between the stitches will gather up, making its overall shape smaller. Gathering can be used as a decorative feature, or to enable you to fit a wide panel of fabric to a smaller one, such as fitting the body of a skirt to a waistband.

A ready-made pattern will have the gathering lines—the lines you sew the running stitch along—marked on it.

Gathering by hand

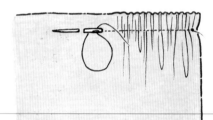

1 To practice gathering, sew a line of small running stitches. Pull the loose end of the thread gently and the fabric will gather up. Use your fingers to distribute the fullness of the gathers to the desired amount. Finish off in the usual way.

2 If you are using gathering for decoration, sew lines of running stitches in even rows and pull all the threads evenly.

Gathering by machine

1 Adjust the stitch length on your machine to the largest straight stitch. Make two or more rows of evenly-spaced stitching.

2 Secure one end of the stitching by winding the threads around a pin, placed at right angles to the stitching.

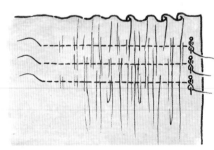

3 At the other end of the stitching, pull the bobbin thread gently to gather, then distribute the fullness of the gathers to the required amount. Finish as usual.

Gathering to fit

1 To gather one piece of a garment so that it will fit onto another piece, first sew a line of running stitches along the edge that needs to be gathered.

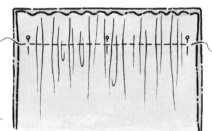

2 Place the two fabrics right sides together and pin at either end and at the center point, placing the pins at right angles to the stitching. Gently pull the thread from each end to the middle, and distribute the fullness evenly.

3 Pin, baste, and sew together the two pieces and remove the gathering stitch.

You'll be putting these techniques into practice in the next project!

Working with curves

Curved edges often need to be snipped with scissors, between the raw edge and the seam, so that the curve can spread and sit properly, without puckering or gathering. The snips or "notches" also eliminate bulk along the stitching line when the item is turned right sides out.

Sewing a straight edge onto a curved edge takes a bit of thought, but with practice, and lots of pinning and basting, it is not an impossible task.

Outward curves

"Notches" allow an outward curve to spread and keep its shape.

1 Using scrap fabric, pin, baste, and sew the seam of an outward curve, right sides together, as usual, leaving a seam allowance.

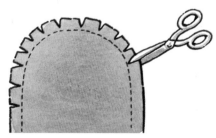

2 Snip out little triangles, cutting from the raw edge of the fabric up to the seam, taking care not to snip into the stitches. You should be left with even-sized "notches."

Inverted curves

Snipping around the edge of an inverted curve allows the curve to spread when the item is turned right sides out.

1 Using scrap fabric, pin, baste, and sew the seam of an inverted curve, right sides together, as usual, leaving a seam allowance.

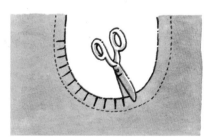

2 Use scissors to just snip into the fabric from the raw edge to the seam, taking care not to snip into the stitches. You should be left with small, straight cuts, evenly spaced apart.

Sewing a straight edge onto a curve

Sometimes one part of an item or garment with a straight edge needs to be stitched to another part that has a curved edge.

1 To practice, take two pieces of scrap fabric. Give one a straight edge and one a curved edge. Lay the curve-edged panel flat and begin to position the straight edge on top. Work slowly, only pinning and basting a little at a time.

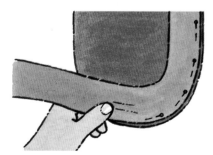

2 Keep easing and gently pulling the straight edge around the curve. Take care not to allow the curved edge to gather. The straight edge will probably need to be snipped to allow it to curve with the other edge.

Slipper selection

I bet you didn't expect to be able to sew footwear, did you? These slippers can be made to fit any foot size, but bear in mind that you will need to buy more fabric for larger sizes—the lengths of fabric specified in the materials list are based on a medium U.S. shoe size of 4 (34–36 U.K.).

This project uses the sewing skills you have already learned. But if you need to be reminded of any of the techniques, simply look back at the illustrations and instructions on the techniques pages.

Native American design

These suedette slippers will complete a great dress-up outfit with the T-shirt that you customized in Project 5.

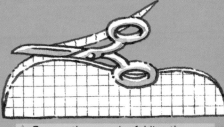

▲ Even up the curve by folding the pattern in half and trimming any excess.

Cutting out the soles

1 Draw, quite closely, around one of your feet onto pattern cutting paper. Add ½ inch (1.25 cm) all around the pattern.

2 Fold the paper pattern in half lengthwise, and trim along the line to make a symmetrical pattern. Step back on to the pattern to make sure it is not too small.

3 On the back of the suedette, draw around the paper pattern twice and cut out two soles. Do the same on the felt.

4 Cut out two soles from the thin batting and the foam, then cut again so they are ½ inch (1.25 cm) smaller all around.

Best foot forward!

Materials

- $^1/_2$ yard (0.5 m) beige suedette fabric, 36 inches (1 m) wide

- $^1/_2$ yard (0.5 m) yellow felt, 36 inches (1 m) wide

- 10 x 15 inch (25 x 38 cm) piece of thin batting

- 10 x 15 inch (25 x 38 cm) piece of $^1/_2$ inch (1.25 cm) thick foam

- $1^1/_2$ yards (1.5 m) yellow bias binding, 1 inch (2.5 cm) wide

- $1^1/_2$ yards (1.5 m) thin brown lacing or cord

- Decorations: 8 hair beads; 4 feathers

- Sewing thread to match fabric

- Strong sewing thread to match fabric for hand stitching, and strong sewing needle

- Sewing machine (optional)

- Scissors and pins

- Tape measure, safety pin

- Pattern cutting paper, pencil, and tailor's chalk

- Iron with various settings

Cutting out the sides

1 Place the end of a tape measure next to the edge of the paper pattern, at the center of the heel. Measure around the pattern until the tape measure gets back to the point it started.

2 Cut two strips each of suedette and felt, the same length as the measurement you have just taken and 3 inches (7.5 cm) wide.

 Carefully cut out the measured rectangle from each fabric strip.

3 On the back of each strip of fabric, mark the center point. Measure 5 inches (13 cm) out to each side of the center. Draw a line between these two marks, 1½ inches (3.75 cm) down from the top edge. Cut into the fabric from the top edge where the line starts, then cut along the line and down from the top edge again where the line ends.

⚠ Carefully cut away another strip from the top side edges of the felt pieces.

4 Take the two felt strips and cut away a ½ inch (1.25 cm) strip from the top side edges.

Cutting out the top ovals

1 Draw a 4½ x 3½ inch (11.5 cm x 9 cm) rectangle on pattern cutting paper. Cut out the rectangle and fold it in half lengthwise. Round off the corners of the folded rectangle, making the lower part slightly narrower at the side. Cut along the new lines to make a symmetrical shape.

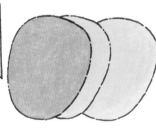

⚠ Pin the pattern to the suedette and felt before you cut it out.

2 Unfold the pattern and use it to cut two suedette and two felt ovals.

Putting together the soles and sides

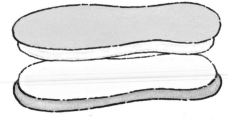

Lay the foam and batting sole on the wrong side of the suedette sole, then place the felt sole on top.

1 Fold the suedette soles in half lengthwise and make a mark at the edge of the sole to indicate the center front and center back—toe and heel. Place a foam and a batting sole on the wrong side of a suedette sole—foam on the suedette and batting on the foam. Lay a felt sole on top.

2 Pin and baste around the edge and repeat for the other sole. Remove the pins and sew the seam, by hand, using a small running stitch, or on a sewing machine. Repeat with the second sole.

3 Put the two suedette side panels together, right sides together. Put the two felt side panels together. Fold down the center front. Mark the center point on the top and bottom edges of each panel.

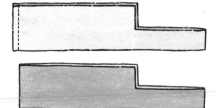

After sewing down the back seams, turn the suedette right sides out.

4 Pin, baste, and sew down the back seams on each piece of the suedette and the felt. Press the seams open and turn the suedette right sides out.

Remember to tell an adult when you use the iron. They may want to supervise, or you could ask an adult to do the pressing for you.

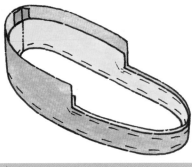

Place the felt panel inside the suedette and baste along the bottom edge and the front lower edge.

5 Position the felt side panels on the inside of the suedette side panels with the wrong sides facing. Match the back seams together and the chalk marks at the center front. Pin and baste along the bottom edge, then pin and baste along the front lower edge.

With right sides together pin in place where the chalk marks meet.

6 Turn the side panels felt side out. Match the back seam to the chalk mark on the heel of the sole, right sides together. Match up the front marks on the sole to the center front mark on the side panel. Pin at the marks.

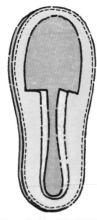

Pin, baste, and sew the side panels onto the soles.

7 Gradually ease the side panel around the curved edge of the sole, pinning as you go. When the side edge fits around the sole, baste, then sew in place. Repeat for the second slipper.

8 Bind the raw edges with bias binding where the side panel joins the sole and turn the slippers right side out.

Finishing the slippers

1 To make the casing for the cord, fold the suedette edge around the heel of the slipper ½ inch (1.25 cm) over the felt edge. Pin, baste, and sew close to the lower edge.

⚠ Remember to leave the thread loose so the toe of the slipper can be gently gathered.

2 Sew a small running stitch, using strong thread, along the top edge of the toe of the slipper, but do not finish off since this is going to be gathered. Now complete steps 1 and 2 for the other slipper.

3 Place a suedette oval, right side up, on top of a felt oval. Pin and baste. Sew ¼ inch (6 mm) in from the edge. Repeat to make a second oval top panel.

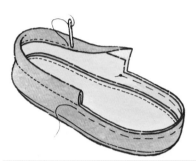

⚠ When you've finished you'll have four marks on your oval.

4 Place each oval on a flat surface with the widest part at the top. Fold across the width, top to bottom. Unfold and measure 1 inch (2.5 cm) up from the fold line, toward the top of the oval. Make a mark at this point on both edges of the oval. Now fold across the length, matching the side marks. Unfold and mark the center at the top and bottom edges. Repeat with the second oval.

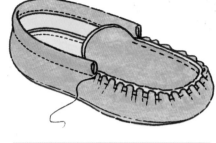

⚠ Gather the toe edge of the slipper before you pin, baste, and sew the oval in place.

5 Fit an oval on the top of each slipper, with the wrong sides together. Match the marks on the ovals to the marks on the sides, where the casing starts. Pin. Match the front chalk marks on the oval and toe, and pin. To gather the toe edge, gently pull the thread so the sides fit around the edge of the oval. Pin and baste in place. Sew the oval in place with strong thread and a small running stitch.

6 To finish off the slippers, make four, evenly spaced, small holes across the front of the oval tops, from the end of the casing to the other side. Thread four beads onto a short length of lacing or cord, and sew a feather on each end. Stitch onto the top of the slipper between the two center holes and the two center beads. Cut the rest of the lacing in half and thread through the casing and through the holes at the front. Tie the lacing into a bow and repeat to finish the pair.

Sparkly slippers

These sparkly slip-ons will make you feel super-glamorous, even when you are just relaxing at home.

Cutting out the soles and sides

1 Use the paper sole pattern you made for the Native American design to cut out sole shapes from the suedette, felt, batting, and foam, remembering to cut the batting and foam ½ inch (1.25 cm) smaller all around.

* all grids not to scale

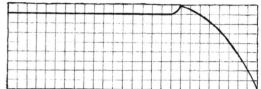

▲ This is the finished shape you will have on your pattern cutting paper.

2 Measure around half the paper sole pattern. Draw a rectangle on pattern cutting paper using this measurement as the length and 3½ inches (9 cm) wide. Measure 3 inches (7.5 cm) in from the right along the top long edge and make a mark. Draw a curved line from this point, down to the bottom right corner. At the other side of the rectangle, measure down ½ inch (1.25 cm) and make a mark. Draw a horizontal line from this mark to a point close to the first mark. Draw a curved line from the first mark down to the line.

3 Use the pattern to cut out two felt and two sparkly side panels. Turn the pattern over and cut out another two felt and sparkly side panels.

4 Cut out four batting side panels, ½ inch (1.25 cm) lower along the top edge and cut ½ inch (1.25 cm) off the bottom edge.

Materials

- ¼ yard (25 cm) pale blue suedette, 36 inches (1 m) wide

- ½ yard (0.5 m) pale blue felt, 36 inches (1 m) wide

- 25 x 15 inch (64 x 38 cm) piece of thin batting

- 10 x 15 inch (25 x 38 cm) piece of ½ inch (1.25 cm) thick foam

- ½ yard (0.5 m) non-stretch sparkly fabric, 36 inches (1 m) wide

- 1½ yards (1.5 m) elastic, ¼ inch (6 mm) wide

- 1½ yards (1.5 m) pale blue bias binding, 1 inch (2.5 cm) wide

- Decorations: length of ribbon for two bows

- Sewing thread

- Sewing needle

- Sewing machine (optional)

- Scissors and pins

- Tape measure, safety pin

- Pattern cutting paper, pencil, and tailor's chalk

- Iron with various settings

Best foot forward!

Putting together the soles and sides

1 Sew together the sole pieces as you did in the Native American design.

▲ Remove the pins and basting after you have sewn down the front and back edges.

2 Take the side panels of the sparkly fabric and, with right sides together, pin down the front and back edges. Baste, and sew ¼ inch (6 mm) from the front edge and ½ inch (1.25 cm) from the back seam. Repeat for the felt and batting panels.

3 Turn the felt side panels right sides out. Place the sparkly panels over the felt, matching the front and back seam. With rights sides together, pin, baste, and sew along the top, ¼ inch (6 mm) from the edge and leaving a ¼ inch (6 mm) gap at one side.

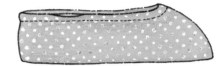

▲ Use a neat running stitch to sew around the top edge.

4 Turn right sides out and press along the top edge. Measure ½ inch (1.25 cm) down from the top edge and pin, baste, and sew all around.

▲ Baste along the bottom edge to hold the batting panel in place.

5 Sew the front and back seams of two batting panels together. Place the batting panel in between the two layers, with the felt on the inside, matching the front and back seams. Pin and baste along the bottom edge.

6 Sew the sides to the soles as you did in the Native American design.

Finishing the slippers

Thread some elastic through the small hole you left in the side seam and gather to fit snugly around your feet. Sew up the ends of the elastic and the gap, and add a ribbon bow on the front.

Now you are the only person to have a pair of slippers for every occasion!

Using paper patterns

You can make your own paper patterns for clothes, toys, and accessories, or buy ready-made patterns from a sewing store. The great thing about working with paper patterns is that you can use them again and again, and you can even adapt clothes patterns to fit different sizes.

Buying patterns for clothes

Ready-made clothes patterns consist of a number of paper pieces in an envelope, with a picture of the finished article on the front. The information on the back of the envelope will tell you how many yards or meters of fabric it requires, and the necessary widths, along with a list of other items needed. It will also suggest the kind of fabrics that are suitable, and say whether stripes, plaids, or diagonal fabrics should be used or not. These details will also refer to the "nap" or "one–way designs," terms that are described on page 15.

Before you buy a clothes pattern, measure yourself and make a note of all the measurements (see Measuring

For Clothes on page 17 to remind yourself of how to do this). Choose simple patterns at first, making sure you pick out the correct size—the sales assistant will be able to help you. If a pattern does not exactly match your size, don't worry. Buy the pattern closest to your size and it can be altered later.

When you get the pattern home, you will see that all the separate paper pieces are for "half of" something—half the front or back, half a facing, one sleeve. Each "half" paper pattern is cut on doubled-up fabric, and the term "place on fold" indicates where you should line up the pattern with the fold in the fabric.

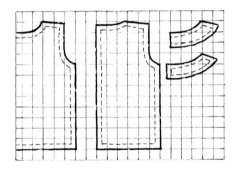

Pattern cutting paper

Cutting your own patterns is a useful skill to learn. If the pattern is accurate you can cut out the fabric knowing that all the pieces will fit together correctly. Your own patterns can also be used more than once.

The easiest way to make your own simple patterns is on pattern cutting paper. This sometimes has a grid marked on it, either in imperial (inches) or metric (centimeters) spacing, to use as a guide. Measure yourself well and transfer the measurements to the paper, adding a seam allowance all around. Make sure you only work in imperial or metric; do not mix the two.

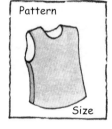

Pattern

Size

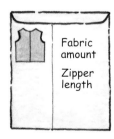

Fabric amount

Zipper length

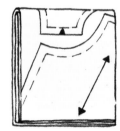

How to make

Altering a ready-made pattern

If you have bought the pattern size that is closest to your own measurements, you should not need to alter it more than 1 inch (2.5 cm) in any direction, otherwise you need the next size up. Make a note of where you need to adjust the size, whether a change to the length of the shoulder to waist dimension, or an increase or decrease to the hip or bust. Always alter the pattern before you cut the fabric.

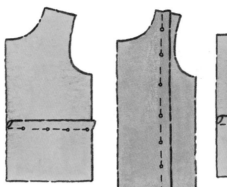
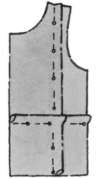

4 By folding and pinning the pattern you can make it smaller. You can shorten it with a crosswise fold, **left**, make it slimmer with a vertical tuck, **middle**, or combine the two for a shorter, slimmer version, **right**. To find out how much to fold, measure yourself and the pattern and fold in the difference between the two.

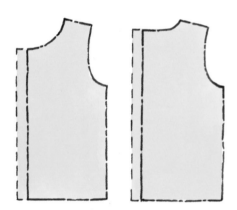

1 If you need to make a pattern larger by 1 inch (2.5 cm) draw a parallel line on the center front and center back of each pattern piece ¼ inch (6 mm) outside the "cutting line." There is usually enough excess paper on the pattern piece for this, but if not, tape a strip of tissue paper to the pattern and draw the line on this. When you cut the doubled-up fabric to this line, you will have added ½ inch (1.25 cm) to the width of the front and back pieces.

2 Make sure you add the same amount to the facing and collar, if you have any.

3 For the sleeves, add ¼ inch (6 mm) onto the side edge.

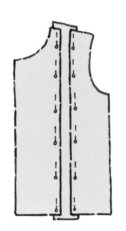
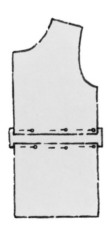
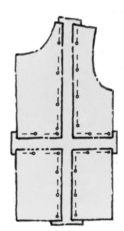

5 Again by measuring yourself and the pattern to find the difference, you can also enlarge the pattern by pinning strips of tissue paper to it. You can lengthen it by cutting the pattern across approximately half way down and adding in the extra measurement then pin the paper strip to the pattern, **left**. Or widen it by cutting the pattern from the middle shoulder, straight down to the bottom edge and adding in the required extra measurement then pin the paper strip to the pattern, **middle**. Or combine the two for a longer, wider version, **right**.

6 For a dress, add the measurements in the same way all the way down the pattern.

7 For a skirt, add to the width in the same way as in step 1, and shorten or lengthen the hem as required.

Tip

To make sure a paper pattern fits correctly before you cut out the real fabric, practice on an inexpensive fabric such as muslin or lining material. Baste the pieces together and make any necessary alterations. Then undo the basting and use this as your pattern.

Lining

Many clothing garments and sewn accessories are lined, which means that the inside is covered with another fabric. The lining for coats, jackets, skirts, dresses, and pants is usually made separately from the garment and sewn in, wrong sides together, after both have been made. Smaller garments can have the lining sewn straight onto the item, right sides together. The lining fabric you use should always be thinner than your main fabric and easy to handle.

If you don't want to put together a whole garment and lining to practice this technique, just read the text and take a good look at the illustrations instead. You can look back at the pictures when you make the next project.

Loose lining

A ready-made clothes pattern that requires a lining will include full instructions for how to make the lining and attach it. You can use these illustrations to back-up your pattern.

1 Turn the finished garment wrong side out and place over a dressmaker's dummy or hang it on a clothes hanger.

2 Place the finished lining over the garment. Pin and baste around the edges, turning in a hem as you go but leaving the hem unattached to the garment. Remove the pins. Sew with a slipstitch. Remove the basting.

Bagged-out lining

Some patterns are lined by sewing the lining and the main fabric right sides together. The pattern will include full instructions, but you may find it easier to refer to these steps as well.

1 Position the lining and main fabric right sides together and pin and baste, leaving an opening in one of the seams. Remove the pins.

2 Sew the two fabrics together using a running stitch. Remember to leave the gap.

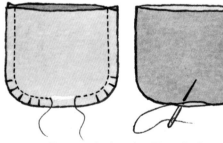

3 Remove the basting. Turn the item right sides out and sew up the gap.

Interfacing

Interfacing is sometimes known as interlining, and goes between the main fabric and the lining. Interfacing is used to stiffen both fabrics and adds durability. You can buy interfacing in various weights. Iron-on interfacing has a shiny back, or has small beads on the back. When pressed with a hot iron, the back surface melts and bonds to the fabric. Sew-in interfacing is pinned, basted, and sewn to the lining or facing. It is important to choose the right interfacing for your fabric, so that both react the same way when washed or dry-cleaned.

Using iron-on interfacing

1 Your pattern will tell you where you need to insert the interfacing—whether to the back of the main garment before the lining, or to the facing—but for now you can practice using it on scrap fabric. Read the manufacturer's instructions, then position some iron-on interfacing on the back of your fabric, making sure the correct surface of the interfacing is touching the fabric.

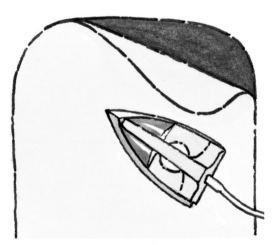

2 Refer to the manufacturer's instructions again to find out which setting you need to have the iron on and how to press the interfacing.

Using sew-in interfacing

1 When you are using delicate fabrics, an iron-on interfacing is not suitable. Sew-in interfacing is placed between a facing or lining and the main fabric. Pin the interfacing to the back of the facing or lining and baste. Remove the pins.

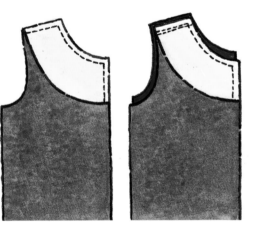

2 Sew the interfacing in place along the edge that is to be sewn to the main fabric, using a running stitch or on a sewing machine. Remove the basting.

Matching sun hat, beach bag, and purse

This cool beach set makes the perfect accessory when chilling out on a hot day. The large bag has plenty of room for all your essentials, and a hidden inside pocket to keep your purse in. The matching hat will protect you from the hot sun's rays, while looking really groovy at the same time.

Don't forget, you can look back to the techniques pages whenever you need help with any of the skills used for this project.

Materials

- 1¹⁄₂ yards (1.5 m) medium-weight toweling, 36 inches (1 m) wide, or a towel of about the same size

- 1¹⁄₂ yards (1.5 m) medium-weight cotton fabric, 36 inches (1 m) wide, for the lining. If you want different colored lining for the bag pocket and hat panels, use 12 x 10 inch (30 x 25 cm) panels for each pattern piece

- 1 yard (1 m) medium-weight iron-on interfacing, 36 inches (1 m) wide

- Decorations: 3¹⁄₂ yards (3.5 m) thick cord; bias binding, 1 inch (2.5 cm) wide, to match the cord; large toggle; 2¹⁄₂ yards (2.5 m) thin cord; small button

- Sewing thread to match the toweling, strong sewing thread to match the cord, sewing needle

- Sewing machine (optional)

- Scissors, pins, tailor's chalk, and tape measure

- Pattern cutting paper and pencil

- Iron with various settings

Beach hat

Making the hat patterns

* all grids not to scale

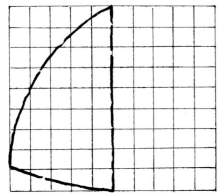

▲ Draw a pattern for the side panels of the hat on pattern cutting paper.

1 For the pattern for the side panels of the main dome of the hat, first measure around your head at the widest part (just above your ears and eyebrows). Divide the measurement by 6. On pattern cutting paper, draw a rectangle with this measurement along the top and bottom edges, and 7 inches (18 cm) long. Draw a center line down the length. From the top of the center line draw a curved line down and out to one side, meeting the edge just over halfway down. Draw a curved line from the center line at the bottom to meet it.

2 Add ½ inch (1.25 cm) seam allowance to the curved lines. Cut along the lines and fold the paper down the center line. Cut around the pattern on the other half of the paper and unfold. Use this pattern to cut out six side panels from the toweling and the cotton lining fabric.

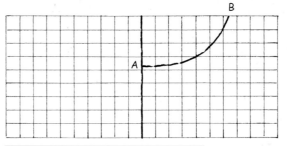

▲ Carefully draw a curved line from "A" to "B."

3 For the pattern for the brim, draw a 16 x 7 inch (40 x 18 cm) rectangle on pattern paper. Draw a center line down the length. Mark 3 inches (7.5 cm) from the top edge down the center line. This is point "A." Measure 3 inches (7.5 cm) in from the top right edge, and mark point "B." Draw a curved line from "A" to "B."

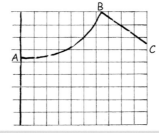

▲ Join "B" and "C" with a diagonal line.

4 Measure 2 inches (5 cm) down from the top right corner, point "C." Draw a diagonal line from "B" to "C."

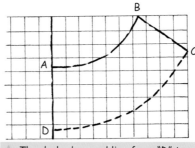

▲ The dashed curved line from "D" to "C" should measure 3½ inches (9 cm) down from the "A" to "B" line.

5 Measure 3½ inches (9 cm) down from "A" and mark point "D." Following the curve of line "A" to "B," make frequent marks 3½ inches (9 cm) down from that line until point "C."

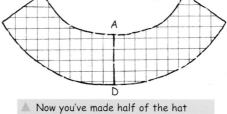

▲ Now you've made half of the hat brim pattern.

6 Cut out along the lines. Fold along the center line and cut out the other half. When you open the pattern you should have a curved half brim.

▲ Add any required extra length by cutting the pattern and pinning in paper as shown on page 89.

7 Measure along the edge from "A" to "B" and multiply by 4 to get your head measurement. If you need extra length add a quarter of this measurement to the fold line "A" to "D." Take off a quarter of the measurement if too long. Add on a ½ inch (1.25 cm) seam allowance at one end.

8 Fold the remaining toweling in half. Place one end of the brim pattern on the fold, pin, and cut out. Repeat with the cotton lining fabric and the interfacing.

Making the hat

4 Repeat Step 3 with the lining brim and dome.

▲ You will end up with two dome-shaped hats, one made of the toweling panels, the other of the lining.

1 Pin, baste, and sew the toweling side panels, right sides together, down the side seams. Start ½ inch (1.25 cm) down from the top. Gradually add on all the panels. Sew the lining panels in the same way, but leave a 3 inch (7.5 cm) gap in the middle of one seam. Press the seams open.

2 Iron the brim interfacing onto the wrong side of the toweling brim. With right sides facing, pin, baste, and sew the two ends together. Sew the lining brim in the same way. Press the seams open.

▲ When you've sewn the two brims together, remove the basting and gently notch the curve with scissors.

5 Lay the lining and toweling brims right sides together. Pin, baste, and sew around the outer edge. Use scissors to notch into the curve all the way around.

6 Turn right sides out through the gap in the lining. Sew up the gap.

▲ Keep your rows of stitching around the brim evenly spaced.

7 Press the brim well. Pin and baste around the brim along the top seam and halfway down the brim. If you are hand stitching, sew a small running stitch around the brim near the top seam. Sew a few more rows down the brim with even spacing between the lines. If you are using a machine, start at the top seam and sew around the seam using the presser foot as a guide for the line spacing.

8 To finish off your hat, slipstitch some cord around the seam near the brim, and tie it in a knot at the front.

▲ Snip into the brim from the raw edge to the seam to even out the curve.

3 Position the toweling brim on the dome of the toweling hat. Match the brim seam to one on the panels. With right sides together pin, baste, and sew the brim around the edge of the panels. Snip into the brim.

Sun time!

Beach bag

Making the bag

1 To make the bag you will need to cut out a 21 x 38 inch (54 x 96 cm) panel of toweling and a 21 x 36 inch (54 x 92 cm) panel of cotton lining fabric. For the pocket cut an 8 x 7 inch (20 x 18 cm) panel of lining fabric, in a different color if you like. You will also need two 3 x 21 inch (7.5 x 54 cm) strips of interfacing.

2 To make the pocket, hem the top of the pocket panel of lining fabric, along one of the longer edges. Turn in a ½ inch (1.25 cm) hem around the remaining edges, and pin and baste.

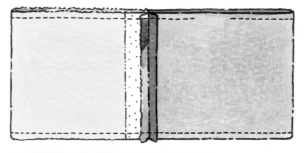

Don't forget to leave a 5 inch (13 cm) gap in the stitching in one side of the lining.

4 Iron the interfacing strips to the two short edges of the toweling panel on the wrong side. Place the lining on the toweling with right sides together and sew across the two ends. Fold the toweling and lining so the seams are together in the middle, and sew down the sides. Leave a 5 inch (13 cm) gap in one side of the lining.

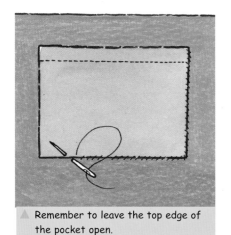

Remember to leave the top edge of the pocket open.

3 Hold the main panel of lining fabric with the shorter edge at the top. Find the center of the top edge and mark 2 inches (5 cm) down on the right side of the fabric. Position the center top edge of the pocket on this mark and pin, baste, and sew onto the lining, leaving the top edge open.

Trim the corner ½ inch (1.25 cm) above the seam.

5 Fold the corners individually on the toweling and lining panel, so the seam is in the center. Measure 2 inches (5 cm) from the point along the seam and sew a horizontal line across the corner. Trim the corner ½ inch (1.25 cm) from the seam. Repeat with the other corner. This will make the corners of the bag less bulky.

Hold the top edge in place by sewing 1 inch (2.5 cm) down the side seams.

6 Turn the bag right sides out through the gap and sew up the gap. Fold the top edge of the toweling in 1 inch (2.5 cm) and press. Sew 1 inch (2.5 cm) down the side seams to hold the top edge in place.

Finishing the bag

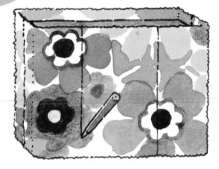

▲ Draw your lines right down to the base and over onto the other side of the bag.

1 Measure 6 inches (15 cm) in from the sides and mark with tailor's chalk down to the base. Measure 4 inches (10 cm) in from the corners on the bottom and continue the line. Repeat on the other side.

▲ Make sure you leave approximately 22 inches (56 cm) length of cord for each of the handles.

2 Slipstitch thick cord along the chalk marks using strong thread, starting from the bottom. When you reach the top edge of the bag, finish off securely and make a loop of cord for the handle, about 22 inches (56 cm) long. Sew the cord back down the other chalk mark and underneath the bag and up the other side. When you reach the top edge, make a handle as before and continue sewing down the other side to the bottom.

3 Finish off the cord by overcasting the two ends together and covering with bias binding. Then sew to the bag.

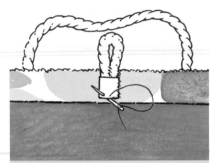

▲ Overcast the loop to the inside of the bag. Make sure the loop is big enough for the toggle!

4 Make a cord loop big enough for the toggle, using the thick cord. Bind the ends together so you have a loop the right size for the toggle. Sew the loop onto the inside of the bag.

5 To finish off, sew the toggle in place on the front of the bag. Mark through the loop for the right position and use a shank for the toggle.

Matching purse

Making the purse

1 Cut out a 9 x 6 inch (23 x 15 cm) rectangle from the toweling, the lining, and the interfacing to form the back panel of the purse. Round off the corners. Cut a 6 inch (15 cm) square of toweling, lining, and interfacing for the front panel. Round off the corners.

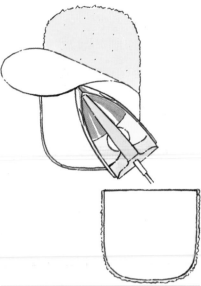

▲ Gently iron the interfacing onto the back and front panels of the purse.

2 Iron the interfacing onto the wrong side of the toweling panels.

▲ Don't forget to leave a gap in the side when you sew up the seam.

3 With right sides together, pin, baste, and sew the lining and toweling front panels along the top edge. **Left** Lay the back panel, right side up, on a flat surface. With right sides together, place the front toweling panel onto the back panel. Pin, baste, and sew up to the seam. **Right** Repeat for the lining, leaving a 2½ inch (6 cm) gap along the side. Use scissors to notch around the curves.

▲ Gently notch around the edges after you have sewn the top of the panels together.

4 Place the right sides of the top of the two remaining back panels together, lining and toweling. Pin, baste, and sew down to the seam. Notch around the curves.

5 Turn the purse right sides out through the gap in the lining. Sew up the gap. Push the lining into the lower part of the toweling purse and press around the edges.

Finishing the purse

▲ Slipstitch the cord to the edge of the purse.

1 Using strong thread, sew thin cord around the edge of the top panel. Start from the side edge 1 inch (2.5 cm) down from the front panel top edge. Leave ½ inch (1.25 cm) from the end of the cord and sew onto the edge of the purse with a slipstitch.

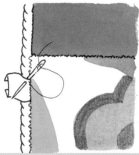

▲ Neatly cover the ends of the cord with bias binding.

2 Hold the ends of the cord together with large stitches. Use bias binding to cover the two ends of cord. Turn in a hem on the binding and sew to the purse.

▲ Use a button shank to sew your button in place.

3 Make a loop of the thin cord long enough to sew to the purse and to fit over the button. Bind the ends together with bias binding. Using strong thread, sew the loop on the inside of the top panel. Mark the button position through the cord loop, and sew the button in place using a button shank.

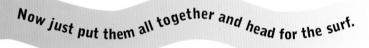

Now just put them all together and head for the surf.

97

Smocking

Smocking is a form of decorative embroidery worked on gathered fabric. Smocking is used mostly for decorating dresses, blouses, and baby clothes. It gives a natural elasticity to fabric, which means it can be used on a wide variety of garments.

It is very important to keep the smocking pleat even and regular. If the initial gathering stitches are close together, you will get small pleats that are suitable for baby clothes. Stitches spaced about ¼ inch (6 mm) apart are suitable for most fabrics, although wider spacing is better for thicker fabrics.

Using smocking transfers on plain fabrics

Spots or checks on patterned fabrics make good guides for the positioning of gathering stitches. If you use plain fabric, however, a smocking transfer needs to be used. These are made up of evenly spaced dots and are available in varying gauges.

1 Iron the transfer onto the wrong side of the fabric.

2 Start at the first dot on the right-hand side, on the wrong side of the fabric. Secure the thread with a good knot and a backstitch.

3 Working from right to left, put the needle in one side of the first dot. Bring it out on the other side. Carry the thread to the next dot and continue to the end of the row.

4 Leave a few inches (cm) of thread at the end of the stitching and repeat the stitching for each row.

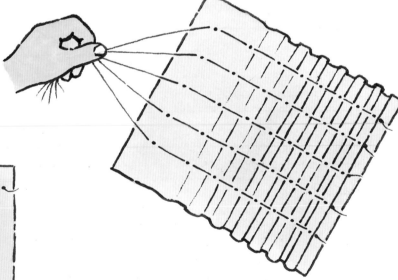

5 Hold all the loose ends of thread and gently pull to gather the fabric. Make sure the fabric is not too tight, but that the gatherings are still close.

6 Knot the threads in pairs so the gathering does not undo.

Smocking on spots

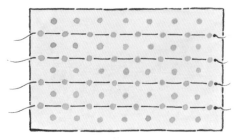

Use a row of spots on patterned fabric in the same way as the dots on a smocking transfer (see page 98). Make sure you only use the rows of spots that exactly align, so that you only use the spots directly under those in the first row.

Smocking on checks

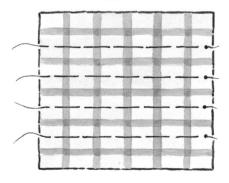

For a dark background to smocking, sew into the center of the pale squares and gather as usual. For a light background sew into the center of the dark squares and gather as before.

Simple decorative stitches

Once the fabric has been gathered, the smocking is finished with decorative embroidery stitches that are often combined to form a distinctive pattern. The running stitches you used to gather the fabric are often used as guidelines for the embroidery stitches. Use embroidery thread and an embroidery needle for these stitches, and work on the right side of the fabric.

Outline stitch

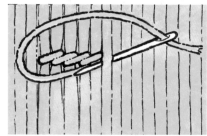

This stitch is used to start most patterns. Bring the needle up to the left-hand side of the first pleat, sew over to the second pleat, keep the thread above the needle, and back out through the middle of the first and second pleat. The needle should point down and come out just under the stitch before.

Cable stitch

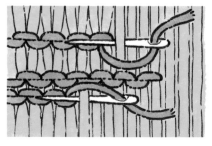

Cable stitch is a firm control stitch and two rows of it at the top and bottom of your smocking can stop the piece from fanning or stretching too much. It can be used as a single line, or in several lines between other styles of stitching to add strength to designs.

1 Bring the needle through to the left of the first pleat on the lower line. Make a stitch through the second pleat with the thread above the needle.

2 Make a stitch through the third pleat with the thread below the needle. Continue across the pleats.

Diamond stitch

This stitch works between two lines of the gathering stitch.

1 Start on the second row of gathering stitches from the top. Secure the thread at the left-hand side and bring the needle through to the left of the first pleat on the gathering line. Draw the needle horizontally through the second pleat with the thread below the needle.

2 With the thread still below the needle, insert the needle horizontally through the third pleat on the upper, first, gathering line. With the thread above, insert the needle through the fourth pleat on the upper line.

3 With the thread above, insert the needle through the fifth pleat at the lower line. Continue to the end of the row.

4 The second row is simply worked in reverse.

Facings

Facings are used to finish raw edges of a garment, such as necklines, armholes, and front openings. A facing is a piece of fabric that fits inside the garment, and can be made in the same fabric as the garment or in a lightweight lining fabric. Facings can add firmness to some thinner fabrics and hold the shape of the garment. Interfacing can be stitched or ironed onto the reverse side of the facing to help stiffen or hold the edge in shape. There are three basic types of facing—bias facings, shaped facings, and extended facings.

Bias facings

A bias facing is a narrow strip of fabric cut on the bias so that it can be shaped to the curve it will finish. It is usually made from lightweight fabric so that it's not bulky. A bias facing should be about ½ inch (1.25 cm) wide when finished.

1 Cut the bias strip twice as wide as the desired finished width. Add a seam allowance of ½ inch (1.25 cm) on both sides.

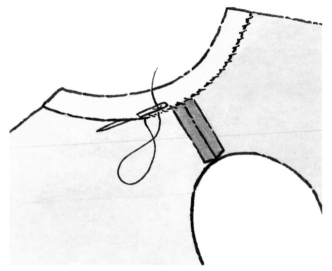

3 Trim the facing seam allowance and snip along the inside curve. Turn the facing to the inside and slipstitch. Trim the ends, folding under ¼ inch (6 mm). Sew up the opening.

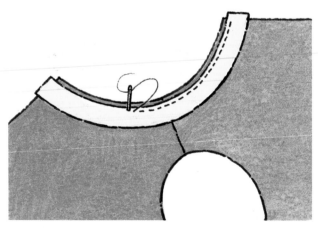

2 Fold the strip in half lengthwise, wrong sides together. Match the raw edges and press along the folded edge. Pin, baste, and sew the bias facing along the neckline of the garment, easing the bias strip along the inward curve and stretching along the outward curve.

Tip

If you don't want to make a whole garment to practice this technique, just read the text and take a good look at the illustrations instead. You can look back at the pictures when you sew the next project.

Shaped facings

This type of facing is a separate piece of fabric cut from a pattern the same shape as the garment edge. If you buy a pattern, all the facing pattern pieces will be included. If you alter a pattern, don't forget to alter the facing pattern as well.

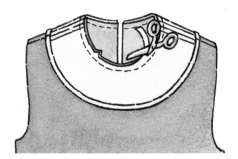

2 Join the separate facing pieces together across the shoulder seams, with a ¼ inch (6 mm) seam allowance, right sides together. Trim the seam allowance close to the stitching.

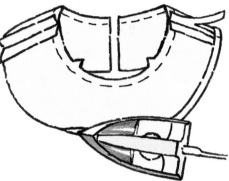

3 Press the seams open. Turn in a ¼ inch (6 mm) hem around the bottom edge and press.

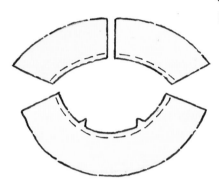

1 To face a neckline, first sew or iron on the interfacing to the wrong side of the facing pieces. Baste around the neck edge of the facings—this is called stay stitching, when used to keep a shape around an edge.

4 Right sides together, place the facing around the neckline of the garment, matching up the shoulder seams. Stitch the facing to the garment with the facing side up. Trim the facing seam allowance narrower than the garment. This helps the edge to be less bulky. Snip around the neckline curve.

5 Press the facing inside the garment. To hold the facing inside, make a few overcast stitches where it meets the seam. This prevents it from working its way out when you wear your garment.

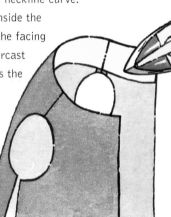

Extended facings

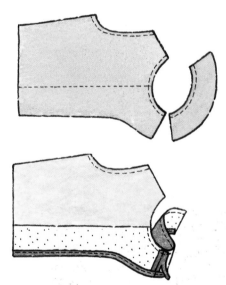

1 An extended facing is cut as part of a front or back pattern along an opening edge. On a ready-made pattern it is included on the pattern piece with a center front or back line drawn on. The facing is cut, continuing out from the center front or back line one third of the pattern shape instead of the whole width, **top**. Attach interfacing to the wrong side of the facing up to the center front or back line, **bottom**. This is where the facing folds back to the inside of the garment. A back neck facing is interfaced and joined to the shoulder seams of the front facing, right sides together. Trim the facing seam allowance at the shoulder seam. Hem the raw edge approximately ¼ inch (6 mm) to the inside of the facing.

2 Fold the facing along the fold line with the right sides together. Match the shoulder seams. Sew around the neckline. Trim the facing seam allowance. Snip and turn right sides out and press.

Smocked halterneck dress

This beautiful halterneck dress is suitable for any party, or just lovely, lazy, sunny days. The smocked front makes it truly exclusive. Your friends and family won't believe it's another fantastic garment you've made yourself!

This project uses the sewing skills you have already learned. If you need to be reminded of any of the techniques, simply look back at the illustrations and instructions on the techniques pages.

Measuring and making a pattern

1 Draw a vertical line down the pattern cutting paper 3 inches (7.5 cm) from the left edge. This marks the center line of the completed pattern. Work from this line when you transfer your measurements to the paper.

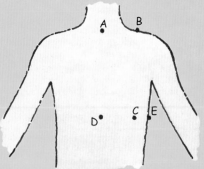

△ Measuring from points "A" to "E" will give you the information you need to make the top part of the pattern.

2 Measure from the middle of your neck, point "A," to the middle of your shoulder, point "B." Measure straight down from point "B" to under your bust, point "C." Measure from the center of your chest, point "D," to the side directly under your arm, point "E."

Materials

● About 2 yards (2 m) light to medium-weight cotton fabric 45 inches (1.15 m) wide, (plain, small dots, simple plaids, or pale floral prints are OK to use)

● ½ yard (0.5 m) interfacing

● ½ yard (0.5 m) thin braid or ribbon to match your fabric or embroidery thread colors

----

● ½ yard (0.5 m) bias binding to match your fabric

● ½ yard (0.5 m) elastic, 1 inch (2.5 cm) thick

● Sewing thread, to match the main fabric

● Embroidery thread, in colors of your choice

● Sewing machine (optional)

● Embroidery needle and sewing needle

● Scissors and tape measure

● Pattern cutting paper, pencil, and ruler

● Tailor's chalk

● 9 x 8 inch (23 x 20 cm) smocking transfer

● Iron with various settings

✱ all grids not to scale

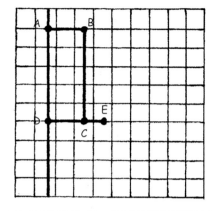

▲ Use your ruler to help keep your lines straight when transferring your measurements.

3 Transfer these measurements to the pattern cutting paper, using the vertical line you drew in originally as the "A" to "D" line.

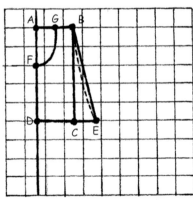

▲ The top part of your pattern is taking shape.

4 Mark point "F," 4½ inches (11 cm) down from "A." Mark point "G," 2 inches (5 cm) in from "B." Draw a curved line from "G" to "F." From "B," draw a line that curves slightly toward the "A" to "D" line, down to "E."

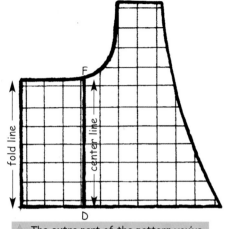

▲ The extra part of the pattern you've added from the center line to the fold line is for the gathering.

5 Draw a straight line out from "F" and another from "D" to the side edge and join with a vertical line. Add ½ inch (1.25 cm) seam allowance all around and cut out the pattern.

6 Place the fold line of the pattern on a fold on the main fabric and cut out the fabric.

Facing pattern

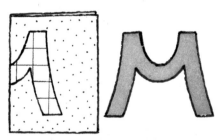

▲ Place the facing pattern on the fold of the facing fabric and cut out. Repeat on the interfacing fabric.

Fold the pattern back to the center line "F" to "D." Place on another sheet of pattern paper and draw around the curved edge, shoulder, and side edge. Remove the pattern. Draw a line 2½ inches (6 cm) in from the first line you drew. This is the facing pattern. Cut it out and place the center line on a fold of the fabric and cut out. Repeat on the interfacing.

Fabulous frock!

Skirt pattern

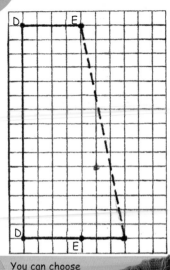

You can choose the length of the skirt!

1 For the lower part of the dress, measure from under your bust down to the dress length you prefer. Use a central line on the pattern cutting paper and draw this measurement down that line. From the top of the center line draw a horizontal line the same length as "D" to "E" of the top pattern made in step 2. Also mark points "D" to "E" along the bottom edge of the dress pattern. Add 4 inches (10 cm) to the side, along this bottom line. Draw a diagonal line from "E" at the top to the end of this line.

2 Add ½ inch (1.25 cm) seam allowance along the top and side. Add 1½ inches (3.75 cm) for a hem along the bottom edge. Cut out the pattern.

Before cutting out the back panel of the skirt, mark the extra measurements with tailor's chalk.

3 Place the central line on the fold of the fabric and cut out to make the front panel of the skirt. For the back panel, place the central line on a fold of fabric and extend the top edge 1 inch (2.5 cm) and the side 3 inches (7.5 cm) from the top to the bottom. Mark with tailor's chalk and cut out.

Straps

For the straps, cut four 26 x 3 inch (66 x 7.5 cm) lengths of the main fabric.

Smocking

1 Match the center of the front top piece with the center of a smocking transfer, and iron on the reverse of the fabric.

2 Sew the gathering stitches with sewing thread on the wrong side of the fabric, working from right to left. Gather to a 3 inch (7.5 cm) pleat width.

3 Choose your smocking stitches and embroidery thread colors and smock down the panel, on the right side of the fabric.

4 Remove the gathering stitches. Sew braid or ribbon down either side of the smocking with a slipstitch, using sewing thread.

Putting together

1 Iron the interfacing to the fabric facing on the wrong side. Hem the inside edge ¼ inch (6 mm) and press.

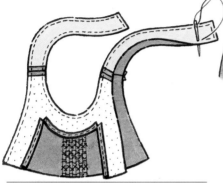

Sew the interfacing and facing around the outer edge of the straps.

2 Pin, baste, and sew two straps to the shoulders of the top front and the facing, right sides together. Place the facing and straps onto the right side of the top and the other two straps. Pin, baste, and sew around the outer edge. Snip around the curved edges and trim off corners.

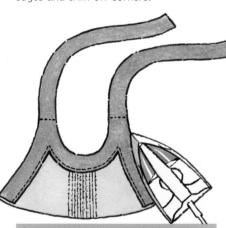

Press gently around the edges of the top when you've turned it right side out.

3 Turn right side out, using a rounded tool such as a knitting needle or round-edged scissors to help push the straps through. Press around the edges.

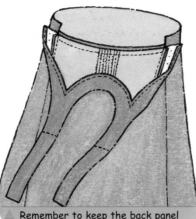

Remember to keep the back panel 1 inch (2.5 cm) higher than the front panel at the top.

4 Pin, baste, and sew the side seams of the skirt panels, right sides together. The back panel is 1 inch (2.5 cm) higher at the top. Press the seams open. Pin, baste, and sew the top, right sides together, to the skirt front up to the seams.

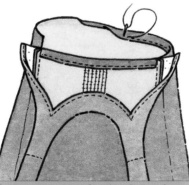

Create a casing for the elastic along the back top edge.

5 Along the back top edge, turn under a ¼ inch (6 mm) hem, then turn down 1¼ inch (3 cm) for the elastic casing. Pin, baste, and sew close to the edge. Press the seam down along the front edge, fold the facings, and baste in place. Bind along the front seams with bias binding.

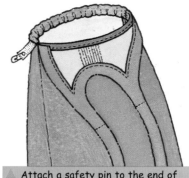

Attach a safety pin to the end of your elastic so that you don't lose it in the casing.

6 Thread some elastic through the back casing and secure one end by overcasting to the seam, then sew up the opening. Pull the elastic to the other end and sew securely to the other seam. Cut off any excess and sew up the opening.

7 To finish off the dress, hem along the bottom edge, turning in ½ inch (1.25 cm), then 1 inch (2.5 cm) toward the inside. Slipstitch along the hem edge.

Well, it may have taken some effort, but aren't the results worth it? Congratulate yourself on a job well done.

Zippers

Zippers are less bulky than buttons or snaps, and so are great for fastening clothes and bags. They can be bought in many different colors and sizes, either closed-ended or open-ended. The next project puts the techniques below into practice. You will also be working with checked fabric, which requires extra care when cutting out patterns.

Tip

You can practice sewing zippers to remnants of fabric or to a garment or bag that has a broken zipper. Or you can simply read the following instructions and study the pictures, then use this information when you come to make the next project.

Zipper foot

When sewing on zippers on a machine you will need to use a zipper foot. This is a one-sided foot that allows the needle to run along close to the seam edge, near the teeth of the zipper.

Zipper in a straight seam

If you are putting a zipper in a center back or center front seam, it will have to be stitched in so that the stitching lines are equal on both sides.

1 After sewing the back or front seam up to the bottom of the opening, baste the rest of the seam together and press open. By basting first you make a sharp edge along the seam allowance which you can center more accurately to the middle of the zipper. Remove the basting and lay the closed zipper in the opening so that the seam edges just cover the teeth on both sides.

Non-concealed zipper

This sewing technique is used for garments where the zipper is a feature and needs to be seen. A bright colored, chunky zipper is ideal for a bag, jacket, or vest.

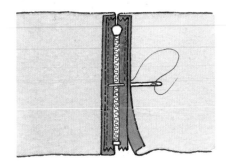
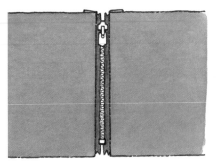
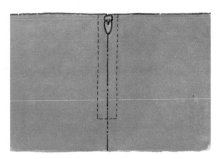

Keep the zipper closed. Place one edge of the zipper, right sides together, along one edge of the garment, matching the seam allowance to near the teeth of the zipper. Pin, baste, and sew along the seam allowance. Sew along the zipper side. Run the stitching evenly down the side of the teeth, if using a zipper foot you will need to use the teeth as a guide. Make sure the zipper is the right way up! Repeat for the other side.

2 Pin and baste the zipper in position. Start sewing about ¼ inch (6 mm) in from the seam edge on one side and stitch down to ¼ inch (6 mm) past the opening. Sew across to ¼ inch (6 mm) past the seam and back up.

Covered or invisible zipper

This is usually found in the center front seam of a pair of pants or the side seam of a skirt.

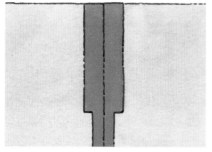

1 For this technique you need to extend the seam allowance where the zipper is placed by ¼ inch (6 mm).

2 Sew up the seam as far as the opening. Press the right side along the seam edge. Fold the left side ⅛ inch (3 mm) into the seam allowance from the seam line and press. This should lie over the right pressed edge.

3 Place the closed zipper under the opening and pin, baste, and sew the right edge close to the zipper teeth.

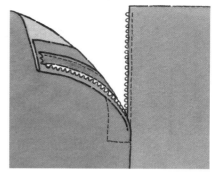

4 Pin, baste, and sew the left side so that the seam edge overlaps the zipper and stitching. The stitching line should be ½ inch (1.25 cm) from the seam line. Sew across the bottom to the seam.

Working with checked or striped fabrics

A little extra care must be taken when using checked or striped fabrics to ensure that the checks or stripes match up when the garment is finished. You can only cut one way and so you will need to use more fabric. Just ask the sales assistant for advice if you are not completely confident.

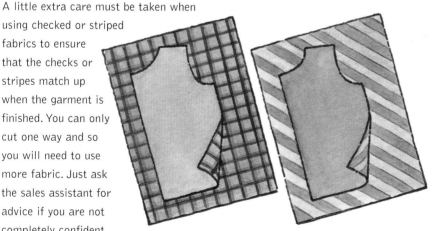

Tip

Try to match up side seams with side seams and shoulder seams with shoulder seams.

▲ Rather than folding the fabric and cutting out the two halves at the same time, when working with checks or stripes it is best to cut one side of the pattern out first. Then pin the cut piece back onto the fabric, matching the check or stripes around the edges as shown above. Turn the pattern over to make an opposite if necessary.

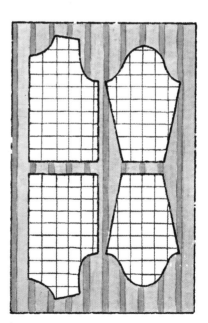

▲ Draw your pattern on a single thickness fabric and reverse patterns on matching checks or stripes, keeping the patterns along the grain line.

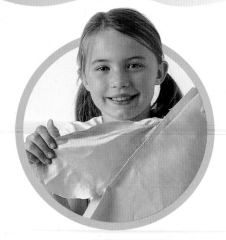

On-seam pockets

On-seam pockets are positioned inside a garment and only their edges are visible—on a coat for example. They are fitted into the side seams of the garment and are usually made of a thin fabric such as thin cotton or a synthetic silky fabric.

Positioning the pocket

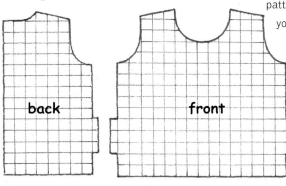

back

front

1 To find a good position for the pockets on a top, put the front pattern side seam against the side of your body. Position your hand where a pocket would be comfortable. Mark the pattern at the top pocket position and also about 6 inches (15 cm) down.

2 Mark the side seams of the back pattern in the same way. Add a ½ inch (1.25 cm) seam allowance along the 6 inch (15 cm) lines on both pattern pieces. Cut out the fabric following the pattern.

Tip

It's probably a bit much to make a garment just to practice this technique, but it's a good idea to read the text and study the pictures before the next project.

Making the pocket pattern

1 Draw a straight line 6 inches (15 cm) long on pattern cutting paper. This will be the open end of the pocket and goes on the straight grain on the pocket lining.

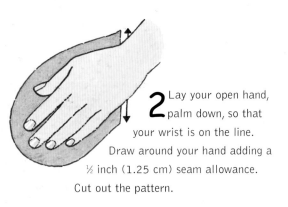

2 Lay your open hand, palm down, so that your wrist is on the line. Draw around your hand adding a ½ inch (1.25 cm) seam allowance. Cut out the pattern.

Making the pocket

1 Use the pocket pattern to cut out four shapes from your lining fabric. These will be linings for two pockets.

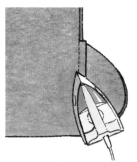

2 Sew each piece to the extra seam allowance allowed in the pattern— one on each of the front panels and one on each side of the back panel. Press the lining and seams outward.

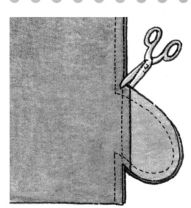

3 Put the garment together and the pocket linings should line up. Pin, baste, and sew down the side seam to ½ inch (1.25 cm) past the top of the pocket lining. Sew around the pocket linings to the seam allowance and then down the rest of the seam. Snip into the curve of the pocket and press the seams open. Repeat on the other side.

Hooded vest

This cozy hooded vest has a colorful, chunky zipper and bright contrasting lining, with a snugly hood and comfortable side pockets. It's made from warm fun fur fabric and will brighten up any dull day, keeping out the cold!

It's a good idea to practice this project first on muslin. Baste the pieces together and make any necessary alterations. Then undo the basting and use this as your pattern. Look back to the techniques pages if you've forgotten anything!

Materials

- 1¼ yards (1.25 m) fun fur fabric, 45 inches (1.15 m) wide

- 1¼ yards (1.25 m) bright lining fabric, 45 inches (1.15 m) wide

- Chunky, open-ended zipper, in a color of your choice: measure from the front of your neck to the length you require for the vest to find the length of zipper you need

- Sewing thread, to match the fur fabric

- Sewing needle

- Sewing machine with zipper foot (optional)

- Scissors

- Pins

- Pattern cutting paper, pencil, and ruler

- Tape measure

- Tailor's chalk

- Iron with various settings

Warm and snugly!

Making the front pattern

1 Draw a vertical line on pattern cutting paper to mark the center front of the vest. Draw a line ½ inch (1.25 cm) in from this line for a seam allowance.

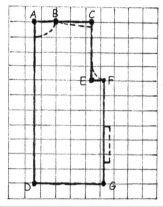

▲ Take measurements from "A" to "E" and make a note of them on a piece of paper.

2 Measure from the center neck straight across to the top of the shoulder—"A" to "B." Measure across the shoulder—"B" to "C." Measure from "A" to the required length of vest—point "D." Measure from "C" straight down to 2 inches (5 cm) below your underarm—point "E."

* all grids not to scale

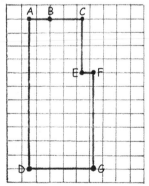

▲ Use the seam allowance line, "A"–"D," as the center front when you transfer your measurements.

3 Transfer these measurements to the pattern cutting paper. Measure your chest circumference and divide by four, then add 1 inch (2.5 cm). Draw

this measurement from the center front seam allowance at the same level as "E"; this will take you to "F." Draw a straight line down from "F" to the same level as "D," to make point "G."

▲ You now have the pattern which you will use for the front panels. You can adapt this for the back panels.

4 To shape the pattern, measure 2 inches (5 cm) down from "A" and draw a curved line from here up to "B." Mark ½ inch (1.25 cm) down from "C" and draw a line that gradually slants up to "B." Measure 2 inches (5 cm) up from "E" and draw a curved line down to "F." Measure 2 inches (5 cm) up from the bottom edge of the vest and make a mark. Mark again 6 inches (15 cm) up from here. Add ½ inch (1.25 cm) between the two marks for the extra pocket seam allowance.

5 Add a ½ inch (1.25 cm) seam allowance all around, but remember that the center line has one already. Add a 1½ inch (3.75 cm) hem allowance along the bottom edge, then cut out the front paper pattern.

Making the back pattern

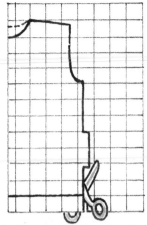

▲ After you have drawn around the pattern, carefully cut it out.

Using your front paper pattern, fold under the "A" to "D" (front center line) seam allowance. Lay the pattern on pattern cutting paper with the center line on another center line. Measure ½ inch (1.25 cm) up from the center back neck and draw a curved line from here to the top of the shoulder. Draw around the pattern and cut out.

Making the hood pattern

1 Draw a rectangle 12 inches (30 cm) wide and 14 inches (35.5 cm) long onto pattern cutting paper.

2 Draw a 2 inch (5 cm) hem allowance down the right side. This is the front edge "A–B."

Tip

Remember that the paper pattern is only half of your finished garment!

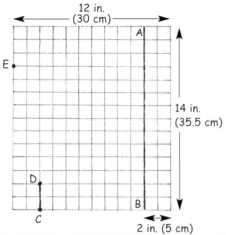

12 in. (30 cm) · 14 in. (35.5 cm) · 2 in. (5 cm)

▲ Transfer the neck measurements to the pattern cutting paper.

center fold line · A · E · D · C · B · front edge

▲ You need to shape the hood pattern before you can cut it out.

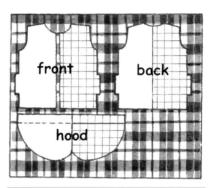

▲ Fun fur fabric is too bulky to cut on the fold. Each pattern piece will be turned over instead.

3 Measure the neck of the back and front patterns to get the neck measurement for the hood. Mark this along the bottom edge from "B" to "C." Mark 2 inches (5 cm) up from "C." This is point "D." Mark 4 inches (10 cm) down from the left top corner to give point "E."

4 To shape the pattern draw a curved line from "B" to "D." Draw a diagonal line from "D" to "E," rounding off the left corner from "E" to the center fold line. Add a ½ inch (1.25 cm) seam allowance at the back and bottom edge then cut out the pattern.

Making the pocket pattern

Draw a straight line 6 inches (15 cm) long on pattern cutting paper. Lay your open hand, palm down, so that the wrist is on the line and draw around the hand. Add a ½ inch (1.25 cm) seam allowance and cut out the pattern.

Cutting out

1 Position the pattern pieces on the back of the fun fur fabric. Make sure the fur is running down the front and back panel. With checked or striped fur, don't forget to match up the pattern sides and front.

2 Draw around the back half pattern then turn it over, keeping the center line lined up with the center chalk line just made. Do the same with the front panel.

3 Draw around the hood pattern making sure the fur runs from the front edge to the back of the hood (as shown above), turn over, keeping the center fold line together. Draw around again. Mark a 2 inch (5 cm) hemline and cut out.

4 Draw around the patterns on lining fabric, omitting the extra pocket seam allowance. Place the back panel on a fold for the center back. Cut the back and front panels 2 inches (5 cm) shorter along the hemline. Place the hood center back on a fold and cut 2½ inches (7.5 cm) lower along the top edge.

5 Cut out four pocket shapes from the lining fabric, using the pocket pattern.

Putting together

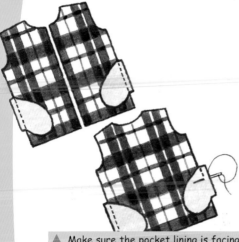

▲ Make sure the pocket lining is facing downward when you pin and baste it along the side seams.

1 Right sides together, pin, baste, and sew the pocket linings onto the side seams of the fun fur vest, along the extra seam allowances. Press the pockets outward.

▲ Sew around the pocket linings but don't sew down where they are attached to the fun fur fabric!

2 With right sides together, pin, baste, and sew the back and front fur pieces together, across the shoulders, down the side seams, and ½ inch (1.25 cm) past the top of the pocket lining. Sew around the pocket lining to the seam allowance and then down the remaining seam. Snip into the curve of the pocket and press the seams open. Push the pockets into the seams.

3 Pin, baste, and sew across the shoulders and down the side seams of the lining panels. Press the seams.

▲ Look at page 106 to remind yourself how to sew in zippers.

4 Pin, baste, and sew the zipper into the fur fabric on the wrong side, using the non-concealed technique.

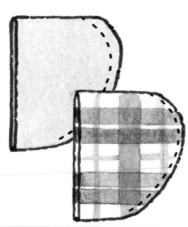

▲ Sew the back seams from the top edge.

5 Pin, baste, and sew the back seam of the hood, right sides of the fur fabric together. Do the same with the lining fabric. Press the lining seam.

6 With right sides together, pin, baste, and sew the top edges of the lining and fur hood together. Press lightly along the seam.

7 Fold the bottom fur edge of the vest, wrong sides together, along the hemline 1½ inches (3.75 cm) in from the bottom edge and fit the lining inside.

▲ Sew around the armholes with right sides together. Start at the shoulder seam and work all the way around.

8 Unzip the zipper. Fit the lining, wrong sides together, into the fur vest. Starting at the shoulder seams, carefully work in between the fur vest and the lining, pinning the right sides together around the armhole seam allowance. Baste and sew. Snip into the seam allowance around the curve.

9 With right sides together, sew along the bottom edge of the vest. Turn right sides out through the side opening. Slipstitch the lining, turning in a ½ inch (1.25 cm) seam allowance, along the side of the zipper, using the stitching as a guide. Repeat on the other side of the zipper.

Warm and snugly!

▲ Sew the fur hood to the neckline of the vest. Make sure you have matched the centers first.

10 Find the center back neckline and match it to the center seam of the fur hood. Pin to hold in place, right sides together. Pin up to the 2 inch (5 cm) hem line originally drawn on your hood (where the zipper and center front should be). Baste and sew. Snip along the seam allowance.

▲ Use a slipstitch to sew the lining in place.

11 Snip the lining along the neck edge of the hood, ¼ inch (6 mm) into the seam allowance. Fold under the hood at the 2 inch (5 cm) hemline. Baste under a ½ inch (1.25 cm) seam allowance and slipstitch along the neckline. Gently press.

Well done! Now put on your vest and zip the zipper. You are ready to brave the cold. Your snugly hood will keep you even warmer!

Darts and waistbands

Darts are stitched folds tapered to a point, the point being at the widest part of the body. They are used to shape and make a garment fit well. Waistbands finish the top of a skirt or pair of pants.

Darts

The width of the dart may vary according to the shape of your figure. With bought patterns all the darts are marked on the pattern pieces and any adjustments may be made during a fitting before the garment is finished.

Darts in a skirt curve at the back to fit the waistband. Measure your waist first and then your high hip, divide the difference by two, and use this measurement for each dart.

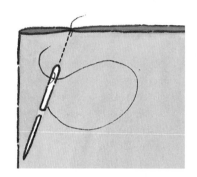

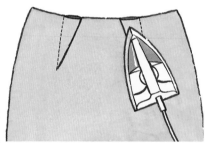

1 The dart should be between the center back and the side seam. Fold down the middle with right sides facing, pin, and baste. The dart should taper out to a point approximately 1½ inches (3.75 cm) to 2½ inches (6 cm) down from the top edge of the skirt.

2 Try on your garment and alter the dart if needed. Darts are pressed flat toward the center of the garment.

Waistbands

Cut a piece of fabric, on the straight of grain, the length of your waist measurement plus approximately 1 inch (2.5 cm) for overlap. The width should be twice the finished width of the waistband. Don't forget to add seam allowances. Interfacing is usually placed along the fold line down to one seam and then the waistband is sewn to the top edge of the garment, along the seam allowance, right sides together.

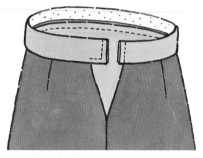

1 After sewing your skirt, place the interfacing side of the waistband, right sides together, along the seam allowance of your skirt. Pin, baste, and sew. Fold the waistband in half, right sides together, and stitch down the ends and along the overlap seam allowance.

2 Snip the corners, turn the waistband right side out, and press the folded edge and ends. Turn under the seam allowance and sew along the inside.

Rosy the ragdoll

These beautiful dolls are a treat to make. You can really have fun decorating them with fabric pens and embroidery. You can go wild with yarn hair using different colors, or add bows and beads. You could even start with long hair and then give it a trim. But be careful as it won't grow back!

This project uses the sewing skills you have already learned. Look back to the techniques pages if you need to be reminded of anything.

Materials

- 1 yard (1 m) cotton fabric 45 inches (115 cm) wide
- Scraps of fabric, ribbon, and colored yarn
- Embroidery silk or thread and an embroidery needle
- Sewing needle and thread
- Tailor's chalk and colored fabric pens
- Buttons for eyes
- Soft batting for filling
- Paper for making pattern and a large piece of cardboard

Making the doll

Draw your own template on a piece of folded paper. Don't forget to add a seam allowance!

1 Fold a large piece of paper in half. Starting from the folded edge, draw half a doll shape as big or as small as you like. Make sure your doll pattern will fit twice onto your fabric. Add ½ inch (1.25 cm) seam allowance all around. Cut around your pattern and unfold the paper. You can always try again if it's not quite right the first time!

Best friends!

2 Fold your fabric in half across the width. Place the paper pattern on your folded fabric. Pin around your pattern and draw around the paper doll. Remove the pins and paper pattern.

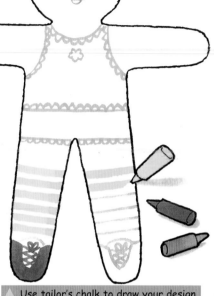

You now have two identical fabric doll shapes.

3 Pin through the fabric around the doll outline. Carefully cut out your doll through the double fabric.

4 Take one of the doll shapes and lay it on a large piece of card. Secure it with tape around the edge, taking care not to tape over the ½ inch (1.25 cm) seam allowance.

Use tailor's chalk to draw your design on your doll if you need a guide.

5 Now for the exciting part— deciding what you would like to draw on the front of your doll. You could practice on the paper pattern first if you want to experiment with different looks. Lightly draw your design on the material with the tailor's chalk then go over it with the fabric pens.

6 Remove the fabric doll shape from your cardboard and take off the tape. Secure your second doll shape in the same way as step 4.

7 Remember this one is the back of your doll. Match up your drawings on both sides by placing the front doll pattern face down on top of the back pattern. Draw matching points around the edge of the back piece.

8 Finish the drawing on the back of your doll. Remove the tape and doll pattern from the cardboard. Fix the drawing by pressing with a medium hot iron.

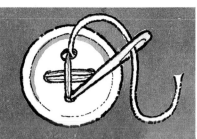

Stitch the eyes on firmly by sewing through the buttons in an "X" shape.

9 Sew buttons on for the eyes. Start on the inside of the doll's face and thread your needle in and out through the buttons in an "X" shape. Go back over this several times and finish off tightly on the inside of the doll to ensure her eyes don't fall off!

Try to keep all your stitches the same length.

Backstitch creates a neat outline for your doll's features.

10 Now for the embroidered features. Using tailor's chalk, draw eyelashes, eyebrows, and a mouth. First sew the eyebrows, using the stem stitch shown at the bottom of the next page. Use backstitch for the outlines of the eyes and mouth. Now fill in the mouth with a simple running stitch and embroider, draw, or sew on a button for a nose.

11 Now your doll is ready to sew. Place one doll shape on top of the other, right sides together, then pin and baste around the edge along the ½ inch (1.25 cm) seam allowance. Leave an opening of 2 inches (5 cm) at the waist of your doll. Then remove the pins.

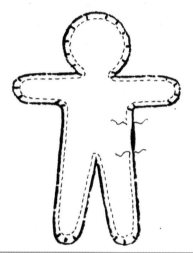

▲ Snipping around the inside corners gives a better outline when you turn your doll right side out.

12 Sew by hand or machine around to the 2 inch (5 cm) opening. Snip carefully around the inside legs, underarms, and neck near to the stitching line, being careful not to cut the stitching. Remove the basting.

13 Turn your doll right side out. Now fill her with batting, using a knitting needle to push the batting

▲ Sew in the middle of the double length of yarn, adding more until you have a full head of hair!

down into the arms, legs, and head. When there is enough padding, sew up the opening by hand.

14 For the hair, cut the yarn you have chosen to twice the length you want the doll's hair to be. Start just above the ear position and, using a few strands of yarn, place them across the seam along the top of her head. Using backstitch, gradually sew across the hair adding more strands as you go. Trim the hair to your desired length.

You can draw underwear, socks, shoes, and jewelry on the front of your doll. Follow the example shown here or have fun with your own designs!

Stem (outline) stitch

This is a very old stitch, which gets its name from being used in embroidery for stitching the stems of flowers!

1 Thread your embroidery needle with suitable thin yarn or embroidery thread.

2 Working from left to right, come up through the fabric at your starting point and make a backstitch.

3 Keeping the thread on the same side of the needle all the time, make another backstitch and bring the needle out right where the last stitch went in.

4 Continue to stitch, always making sure you come back up in the same hole as the end of the previous stitch.

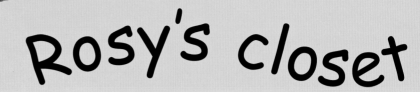

Rosy's closet

Here are some clothes you can make for Rosy the ragdoll. This project is great for using up scraps of braid, ribbon, and lace with buttons and beads to decorate. You can practice your new sewing skills, and learn a few more. And since you know how to measure yourself, you could also scale up these easy patterns and make some more clothes for yourself.

You have learned so many sewing skills that it would not be surprising if you need a reminder of some of the techniques used here. Take a quick look at the relevant technique and you will soon remember what to do.

Measuring the doll

Use this diagram to help you decide how much fabric you will need for each garment. Allow an extra 2 inches (5 cm) all round to ensure you have enough material.

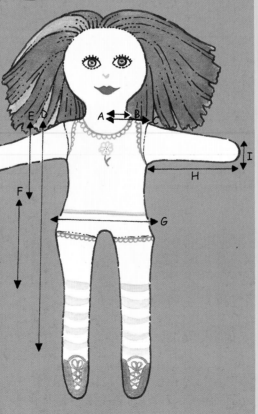

A–B Center neck to top of shoulder

A–C Center neck to shoulder

D Length of doll

E Length of shoulder to waist

F Length of waist to skirt length

G Width of doll

H Length of arm

I Width of arm

Smock top and pleated skirt

As you make this cute combination of smock top and contrasting pleated skirt you will be practicing making darts and adding a waistband. It is easy to make this to fit you, so go ahead, make one for yourself!

Measuring and cutting out

1 For the top, measure from the shoulder to the waist. Cut two pieces of checked cotton fabric to the desired length of the top, adding a 1 inch (2.5 cm) hem allowance. For the width, cut each piece twice the width of the doll's chest measurement.

Catwalk collection!

Project 15

Materials

FOR THE SMOCK TOP

- Checked cotton fabric: 4 x width of the doll's chest and enough for desired length; strip wide enough for the double width and length of the straps

- 2 small buttons or beads

- Embroidery needle and thread

- Sewing needle and thread

- Sewing machine (optional)

- Scissors and pins

- Tape measure

- Tailor's chalk

- Iron with various settings

FOR THE SKIRT

- Plain cotton fabric: long enough to go around the doll's hips, add 4 inches (10 cm) to the width and 3 inches (7.5 cm) to the length

- Checked cotton fabric, the same as the smock top fabric, for the pleat: about 5 inches (13 cm) wide and the length of the skirt

- Small button or bead

- Small snap

2 For the straps, cut two lengths of checked fabric that are twice the required width. Add a ½ inch (1.25 cm) seam allowance to the width. Make sure the length is long enough to go over the doll's shoulders and overlap by ½ inch (1.25 cm) at the front and back of the dress.

3 For the skirt, measure the hips of the doll and add 4 inches (10 cm) to the width. Measure the length you require and add 1 inch (2.5 cm) for seam allowance. Transfer the measurements onto your plain fabric and cut out. Cut out a waistband

● ● ● ● ● ● ● ● ● ● ● ●

Making the smock top

1 To hem the top and bottom of the front and back panels of checked fabric, turn under ¼ inch (6 mm) twice, and sew.

2 Sew gathering stitches into the checks, starting about ½ inch (1.25 cm) in from the edges. You need about six rows of gathering. Gather the panel to the width of the doll's chest.

3 Choose two or three smocking stitches to decorate the front and back of the top. Look back to the technique to refresh your memory.

4 Sew up the side seams, right sides together, with a ½ inch (1.25 cm) seam allowance, leaving a 1 inch (2.5 cm) gap at the top. Sew the seam allowance toward the inside along the 1 inch (2.5 cm) gap at the top. Press.

5 Fold the shoulder straps in half down the length, right sides together, and round off one end. Sew down the side and rounded end. Notch into the curve, turn right sides out, and press.

double the finished width and the waist measurement for the length, adding on ½ inch (1.25 cm) seam allowance all around.

4 Cut out a pleat from the check fabric, about 5 inches (13 cm) wide and the length of the skirt.

6 Put the top onto the doll and pin the shoulder straps in position at the back inside edge.

Mark the position for your buttons by overlapping the straps.

7 Overlap at the front and mark the position for the buttons.

8 Take the top off the doll and sew the straps to the back on the inside of the top edge. At the front, sew the buttons through the strap onto the outside top edge.

Making the pleated skirt

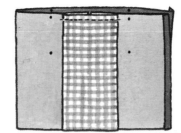

Mark the dart positions on either side of the pleat on the reverse side.

Sew the waistband onto the top of the skirt, don't forget, right sides together!

Baste the folds along the top to make the pleat.

1 Mark a vertical line a quarter of the width in from the side edge. Cut along this line. This is the center front of the skirt. Sew the checked pleat fabric to the center seams of the plain skirt panel, right sides together. To make the pleat, mark the center of the check fabric. Fold the two seams into the middle and baste the folds along the top.

Press the folded pleat and seams well.

2 Press the folded edges down the center and the pleat at the back. Sew up the skirt's side seam, right sides facing, and leave a 1½ inch (3.75 cm) gap at the top. Press the seam open.

3 Lay the skirt wrong side out with the pleat in the center. Mark the center of each panel to either side of the pleat, at the top. Mark the same points at the back, along the top inside edge. Make a new mark 1½ inches (3.75 cm) down from each mark. These points are the top and bottom of each dart.

4 Fold the waistband lengthwise, right sides together, and sew down each end, with a ½ inch (1.25 cm) seam allowance. Turn right side out and press.

5 Measure the length of the waistband and across the top edge. Divide the difference by four to get the measurement for each dart. On the wrong side, mark half the dart measurement either side of the top of the dart with a vertical pin.

Don't forget to remove all the pins before pressing the darts toward the center.

6 Fold the position of the dart, right sides facing, down to the lower mark. Match the pins at the top, pin, baste, and sew from the top mark to the bottom mark. Don't forget to remove all pins! Press the darts toward the center, front and back.

7 Turn the skirt right side out and pin, baste, and sew the waistband to the seam allowance along the top edge, right sides together.

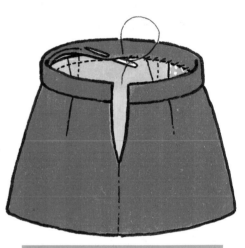

Finish off the waistband by slipstitching along the inside edge.

8 Press along the waistband seam. Turn the waistband to the inside, turn under a ½ inch (1.25 cm) hem and slipstitch along the inside waistband.

9 To finish the skirt, turn under the bottom edge ½ inch (1.25 cm) twice to make a hem. Press the hem, pleat, and waistband well. Sew the snap in place so that the waistband overlaps at the top. Then sew a decorative button or bead on the outside of the waistband, at the same position as the snap.

Catwalk collection!

Materials

- ½ yard (0.5 m) cotton fabric, your choice of color and pattern, 36 inches (1 m) wide.

- 30 inches (76 cm) of narrow ribbon

- Sewing thread to match the color of the fabric

- Sewing needle

- Sewing machine (optional)

- Scissors and pins

- Tape measure

Flower shift dress

This pretty dress is a simple but stylish addition to your doll's closet!

Making the dress

1 Measure across the middle of your doll and add 2 inches (5 cm) to the width. Measure the length for the dress and add 1 inch (2.5 cm). Cut two rectangles of fabric to these measurements.

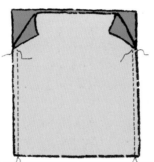

Leave a 2 inch (5 cm) gap at the top on both sides.

2 With right sides together, pin and baste down each side, ½ inch (1.25 cm) in from the edge of the fabric. Leave a 2 inch (5 cm) gap at the top on both sides.

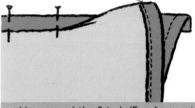

Hem around the 2 inch (5 cm) gaps at the top for a neat finish

3 Turn in a ½ inch (1.25 cm) hem and sew all the way around the two gaps at the top. These are the armholes. Turn over a ¼ inch (6 mm) then a ½ inch (1.25 cm) hem for each of the top edges and sew. Turn up a ¼ inch (6 mm) then a ½ inch (1.25 cm) hem on the bottom edge and sew it.

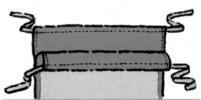

Take your two lengths of ribbon and thread one through each of the hems.

4 Thread a length of ribbon through the hem at the top and gather it to fit your doll. Tie bows at either side. Turn the dress right side out.

Now that you know how easy it is, why not make more dolls as gifts for friends? You could make a whole family of them, or copy the hair and style of your favorite pop stars and make your own girl band!

Oh no! What's gone wrong?

Don't worry if you make mistakes when sewing; most of them can be corrected, and any mistake can be learned from. Read instructions carefully before you begin, to avoid obvious mistakes. Ask someone for help if you don't understand an instruction. Practice on spare fabric first, and make a pattern out of muslin to see if any alterations are needed before you cut into your main fabric.

Getting help

Ask the people around you, family members, friends, teachers, and the staff in your local craft store for help or advice. Often people have their own tips, and probably even some stories of the mistakes they have made.
Here are a few common problems that may occur.

Oh no! I've run out of fabric

Make sure you carefully work out how much fabric is needed before you begin. If you are working from a purchased pattern, read the back of the pattern envelope for the amount of fabric needed. If you are using your own pattern ask in the fabric store for advice on how much fabric to use. It's worth buying extra fabric, if you can, to allow for mistakes—you can always use it to make doll clothes.

Before you cut out any fabric pieces, fit each pattern piece onto the back of your fabric, making sure any pile or nap runs in the same direction on each pattern piece. If there is not enough room for all the pieces, try placing them in a different order on the fabric, and remember that some pieces need a double width. You could use a similar fabric in a contrasting color for facings, pockets, or part of your garment, if there is still not enough of the main material.

Oh no! I've sewn the wrong pieces together

If you make an item and there is a piece the wrong way around, carefully undo the stitching and pin the pattern pieces back together the right way!

Name each pattern piece so you can check that you have all the pieces for the item you are making.

Tip

Remember, most mistakes are repairable.
Don't be in a hurry to cut fabric out without checking patterns, sizes, and measurements first.

Oh no! I've run out of thread

You don't want to work with a thread length that is too long because it will get knotted while sewing. But if you are hand sewing a long seam you may run out of thread. So, if you do run out of thread while sewing, stop and remove the needle.

Machine sewing

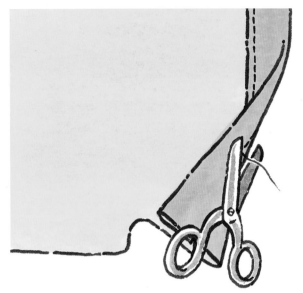

1 If you are using a sewing machine and the bobbin thread runs out, stop sewing, remove the fabric, and trim off excess threads.

Hand sewing

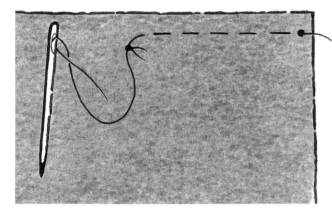

1 If there is a length of thread left, tie the end of a new length of thread to the end of the first thread, close to the last stitch (on the wrong side), and continue to sew with this thread.

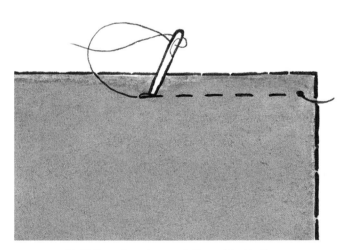

2 If there is not enough thread to tie the new thread onto, simply rethread the needle with new thread and use this to sew a small overcast stitch over the last stitch to secure the previous thread. Continue to sew as normal.

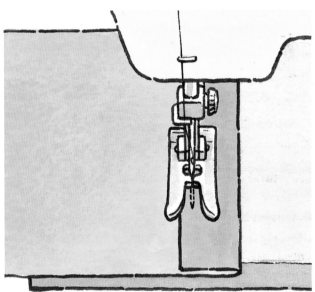

2 Refill the bobbin and place the fabric back under the presser foot at the end of the last stitch. Sew a few stitches back, then continue to sew as normal.

3 Trim off excess thread. If the top thread runs out repeat the instructions but rethread the top thread.

Oh no! My seams are pulling and puckering

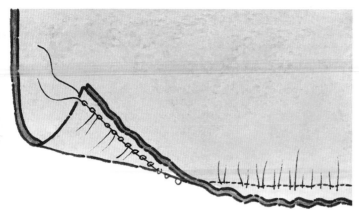

1 Check the stitch tension. If you pull the thread too tight while you are sewing, the seam will not lie flat. The stitches need to be gently pulled so they are not too loose but still hold the seams together firmly. If this happens using a sewing machine, check the tension of the top thread and the bobbin. Practice on a spare piece of fabric (the same as the fabric you are going to use) to get the stitching just right.

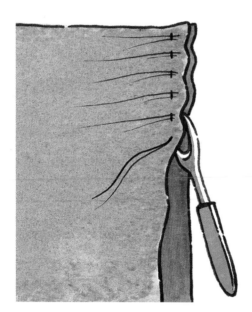

2 If the stitching is pulling and puckering too much, use a seam ripper to gradually remove the stitches, being careful not to nick the fabric. Pin and baste the seam again and re-sew along the seam allowance, taking particular care not to pull the stitches too tightly this time.

Oh no! It doesn't fit

Before you start make sure you measure yourself well, using the diagram on page 17 and writing down your list of measurements on paper. Transfer the required measurements onto pattern cutting paper carefully when making a pattern. Make the garment out of calico or cheap cotton, if you can, basted together, to get a correct fit. (You do not have to finish off hems, etc.) Trim the seam allowance, undo the seams, and alter your paper pattern to the size of the calico or cheap cotton pattern.

If your paper pattern is too big or too small have a look at page 89, which has information on altering patterns.

Have a fitting before you finish any garment, so alterations can be made more easily. Get someone to help you with the fitting, it will be a lot easier!

Oh no! My hem and lower edge is uneven

Make sure you pin all matching seams well, starting from the top and keeping the garment on a flat surface. Lay the seams together and gradually pin along the seam allowance without stretching either side of the garment. Check over the garment after you have pinned. If the hem or bottom edge is not the same length, see if the seam looks puckered, and, if so, undo and re-pin.

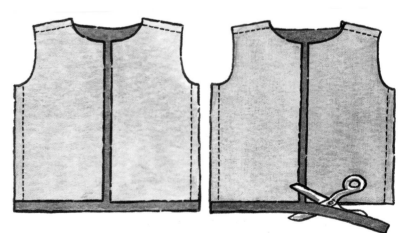

You may need to lay the paper pattern back on the fabric pattern pieces to check that you have cut the fabric out to the correct size, and trim off excess fabric if you need to.

Glossary of sewing terms

Basting

A continuous row of long hand stitches holding two or more layers of fabric together, usually before final sewing.

Ease

Help the fabric edge by slightly pulling or pushing one edge onto the other along a seam.

Facing

To finish a raw edge with a matching shape to fit inside a garment.

Grain

Lengthwise, or warp threads running parallel to the selvage. Crosswise, or weft threads running across the fabric from selvage to selvage.

Interfacing

Fabric inserted between the facing and the garment to support an edge and hold a shape. Interfacing can be iron-on or sew-in.

Marking

Showing seam allowance for cutting. Showing fitting corrections. Any mark made with tailor's chalk.

Nap or pile

Fibrous surface on the right side of the fabric.

Notch

Small "V" cut in the seam allowance to get rid of bulk in an outward curving seam.

One-way fabric

A fabric that has a pattern, nap, or pile running in the same direction on the right side.

Press

To iron the fabric, choosing the right setting.

Pile

Raised woven-in surface on fun fur and velvet fabrics.

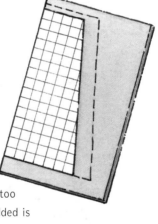

Seam allowance

The extra amount added to the stitching line so that your stitches are not too close to the cut edge. The usual amount added is ¼–¾ inch (6 mm–2 cm).

Selvage

The uncut side edges of the fabric.

Snip

A small cut made up to the seam allowance to enable the seam to spread and follow a stitched inward curve.

Stay-stitching

A line of stitches made by hand or machine to prevent stretching.

Top-stitching

A line of stitches made on the outside of the finished garment parallel to an edge, seam, or other stitching.

Index

Credits

Quarto would like to thank Hettie Reatchlous, Tattie Reatchlous, Ayse Khan, Stephanie Waller, Kaye O'Doherty, Sean O'Doherty, Daisy Savory, Rosie Froud, and Brodie Clark for modeling the projects in this book.

All photographs and illustrations are the copyright of Quarto Publishing plc. While every effort has been made to credit contributors, Quarto would like to apologize should there have been any omissions or errors.

Author's acknowledgments

Thanks to my mom, grandma, Spanish auntie, and all my creative relatives and friends for teaching me how to sew and encouraging me to be creative. This valuable skill has been passed down through many generations in our family and I hope that my daughter Olive will enjoy sewing and making things as much as I have!